Praise for *Hotel Almighty*, by Sarah J. Sloat

2020 AIGA Winner: 50 Books | 50 Covers

***The New York Times Book Review*, "New & Noteworthy Poetry"**

"This book of erasure poems uses Stephen King's *Misery* as its source text, highlighting themes of captivity and imagination. Sloat reproduces the original pages she used, adorned with fanciful collages on the erased sections."

—*The New York Times Book Review*

"Sarah J. Sloat's debut poetry collection, *Hotel Almighty*, is a visual feast. This assemblage of erasure poems and full-color collages is a fantastical, Rubik's Cube of a delight."

—Kelly Fordon, *New York Journal of Books*

"Sarah J. Sloat's *Hotel Almighty* . . . goes all out with erasure and mixed-media collage to reimagine Stephen King's Misery."

—Barbara Hoffert, *Library Journal*

"*Hotel Almighty* is a collection full of possibility and surprise. Of yes, misery and confinement, but also of playfulness and hope. It's worth noting how unusual and thrilling it is to encounter a book of poems infused with so much color. The sophistication of the erasure pairs with the illustrative nature of collage to create a distinct mood, at times, like a subversive picture book for the Future Adult version of the kid drawing in the back of the room, who is too smart or dark or witty for the rest of the class."

—J. M. Farkas, *The Rumpus*

"More in the spirit of play than protest, S. Jane Sloat creates poetry from prose, reconstituting the words and world of Stephen King's *Misery*. Sloat finds dreamy delight in King's suspenseful tale: 'In an act of imagination / late at night. / He threw back his head and / a variety of strange and poisonous flowers grew.' These lines feel like they speak to the creative process in general and to this book in particular.

Each page is a poem revealed through erasure, strange word-flowers growing up from crayons, collage fragments, and loose threads that suggest a feminine hand."

—Kelsey Ervick, *Electric Literature*

"Sloat's brilliant erasures . . . are visual delights that transcend confinement."

—Anna Duke Reach, *Kenyon Review*

CLASSIC CRIMES

CLASSIC CRIMES

Sarah J. Sloat

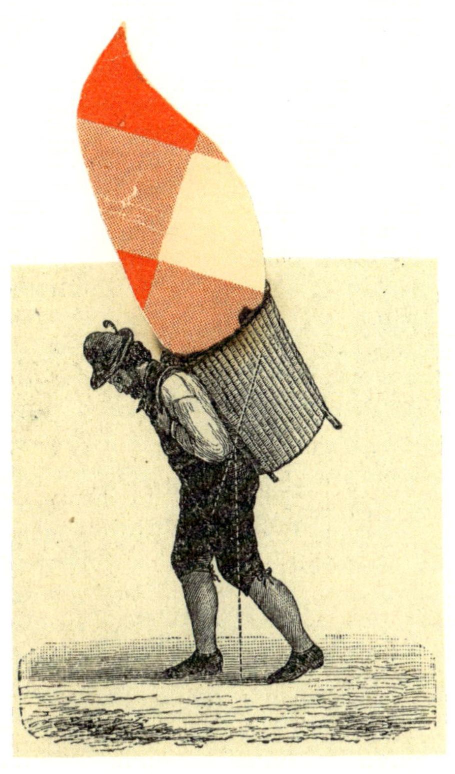

SARABANDE BOOKS
Louisville, KY

First Edition

Library of Congress Cataloging-in-Publication Data
(Provided by Cassidy Cataloguing Services Inc.)

Names: Sloat, Sarah J., author. | Roughead, William, 1870-1952. Classic crimes.
Title:Classic crimes / Sarah J. Sloat.
Description: First edition. | Louisville, KY : Sarabande Books, [2025]
Identifiers: ISBN: 978-1-956046-39-7 (paperback) | 978-1-956046-40-3 (ebook)
Subjects: LCSH: American poetry. | LCGFT: Erasure poetry. | Visual poetry. | Poetry.
Classification: LCC: PS3619.L635 C53 2025 | DDC: 811/.6--dc23

Cover and Jacket by Jessa Dupuis.
Interior design by Danika Isdahl.

Printed in USA.
This book is printed on acid-free paper.
Sarabande Books is a nonprofit literary organization.

Page 1: Quote from the "Adagia" by Wallace Stevens, published in *Poetry* (1957).

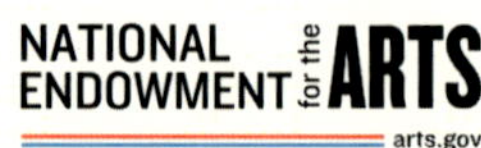

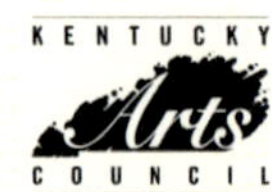

This project is supported in part by an award from the National Endowment for the Arts. The Kentucky Arts Council, the state arts agency, supports Sarabande Books with state tax dollars and federal funding from the National Endowment for the Arts.

For my mother, Lois Cartwright

1936–2025

CONTENTS

DRIVING UNDER THE INFLUENCE

DISTURBING THE PEACE

CLASSIC CRIMES

It is not every day that the world arranges itself in a poem.

Wallace Stevens

SECRETAIRE

Dark-lantern, join the shining:
an epoch's over, it kicked a sick bed
through the dim minutiae of several cities.

Listen: whispering has left the house.
The humming that seduced the theater
became vapor at the stable door.

Break the silence with your singing.
Lift the nightdress from carriage wheels.
Now the neglect of dancing

comes undone, and our application
to be destroyed by fire arrives
in the high court of the connoisseur.

DISORDERLY CONDUCT

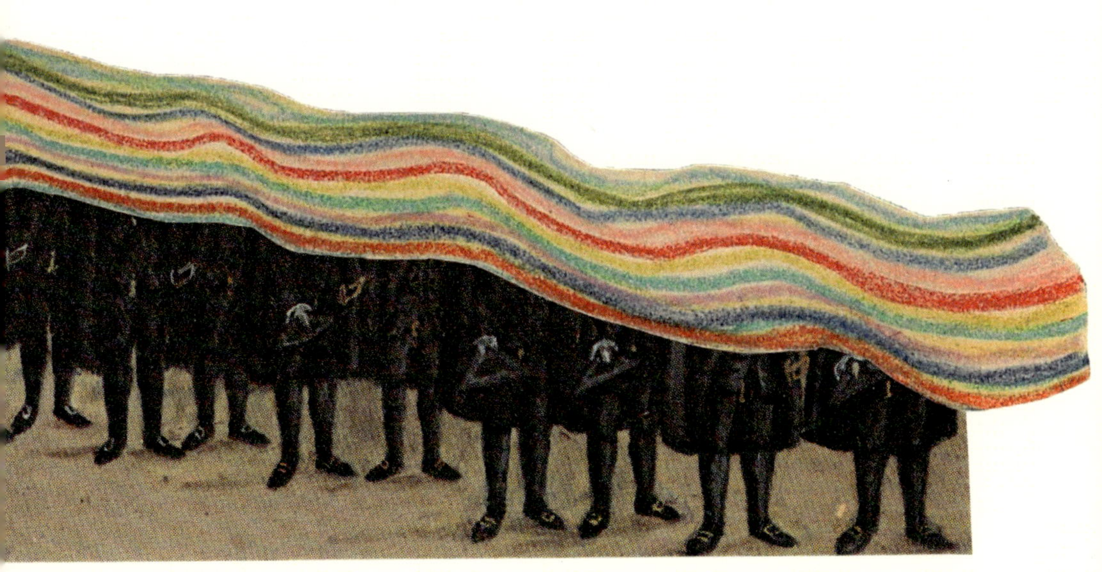

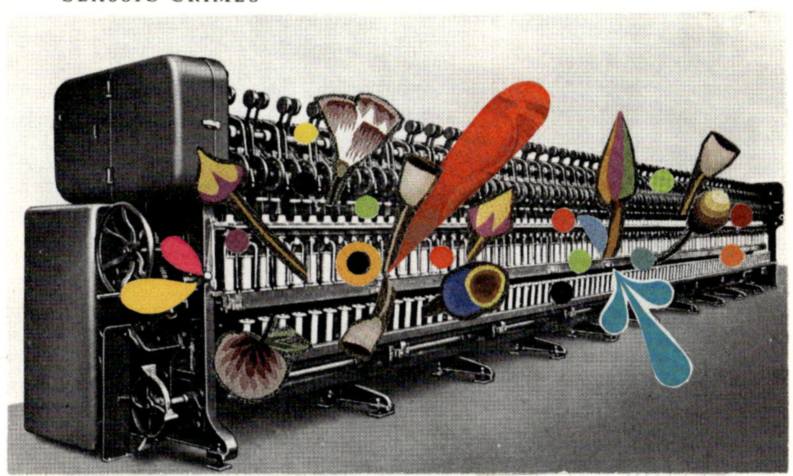

When the

mind

opened

the guests
were mostly birds

the mustaches of
scoundrels
like the fabled Upas Tree of Java,
with its baleful shade
gloried in
victims,
and looked
for mischief
upon
the
nakedness of the land

pleasure.

should

keep in touch with
business

as

mirth and revelry

look for a policeman,

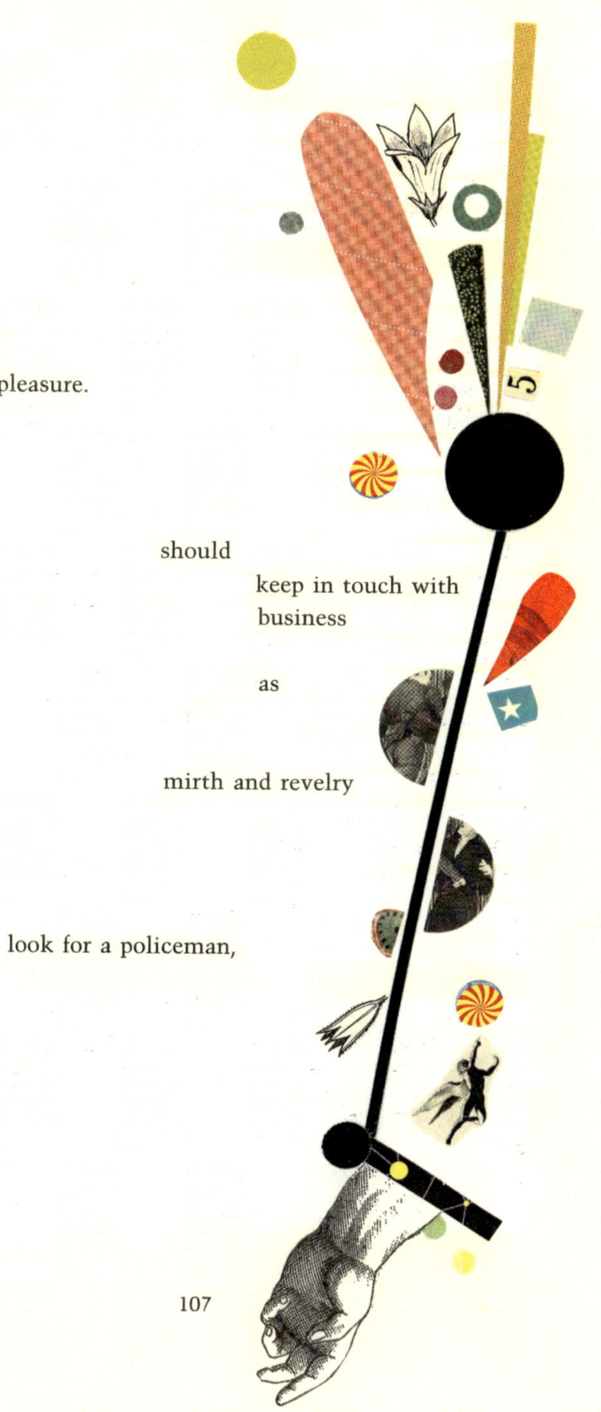

107

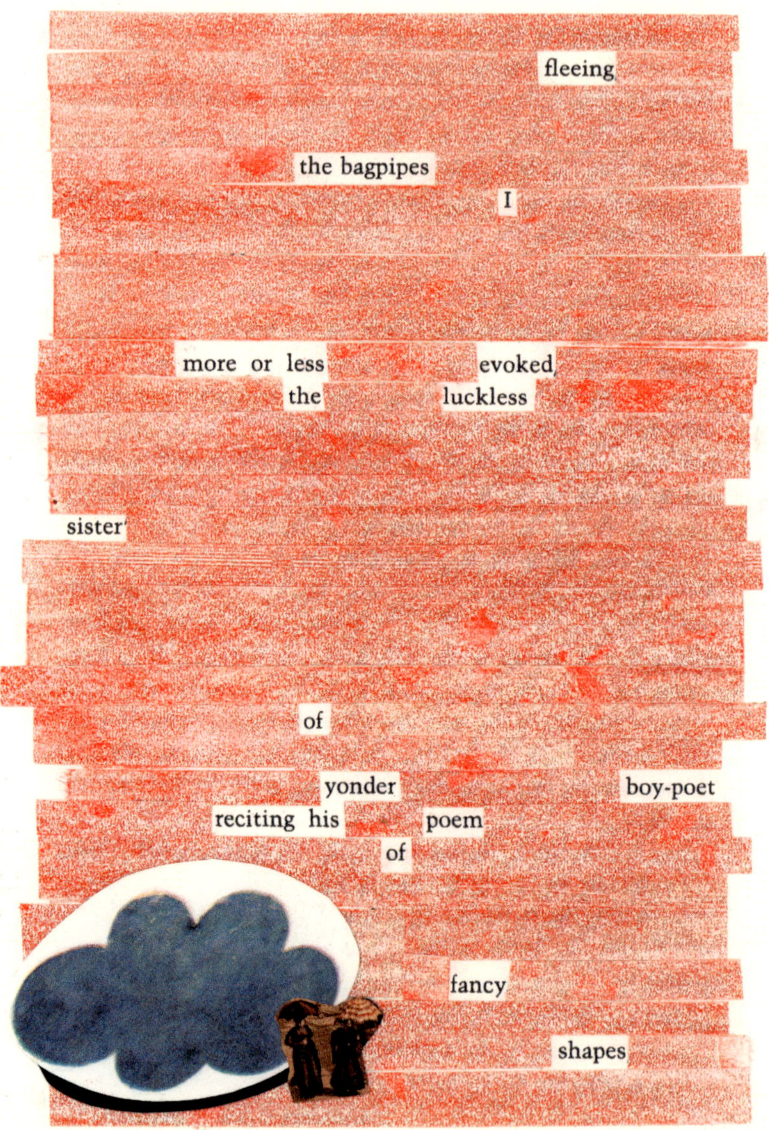
fleeing
the bagpipes
I
more or less evoked
the luckless
sister
of
yonder boy-poet
reciting his poem
of
fancy
shapes

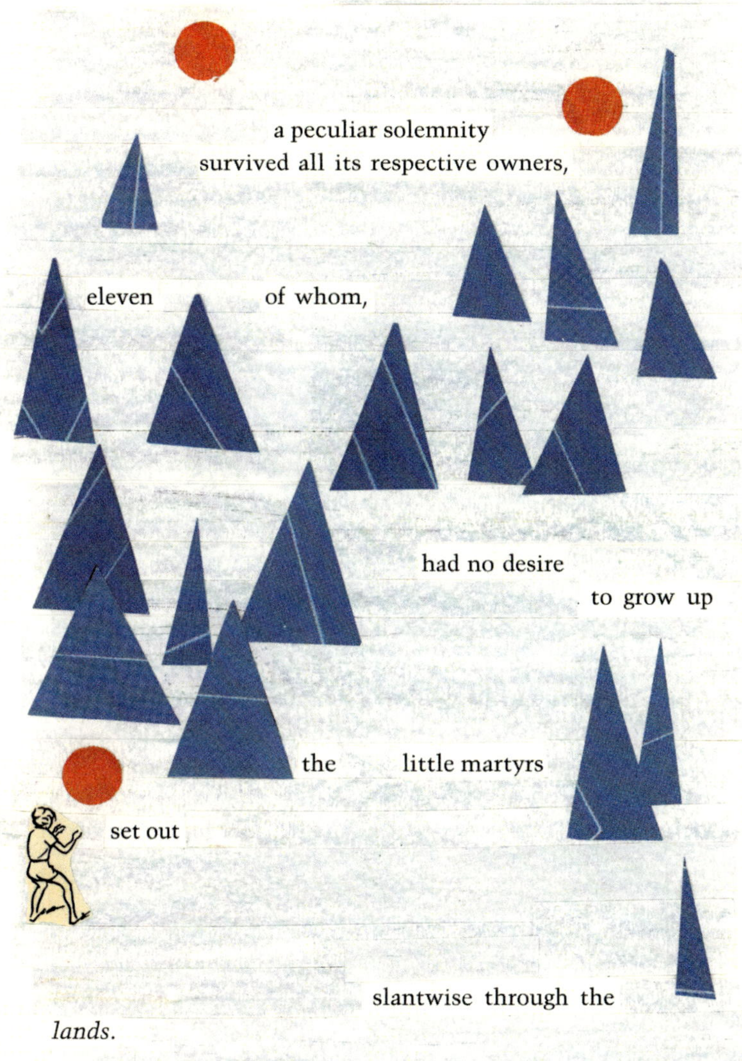

a peculiar solemnity
survived all its respective owners,

eleven of whom,

had no desire
to grow up

the little martyrs
set out

slantwise through the
lands.

39

describe a

friend

affectionately

for an hour

a

day .[3]

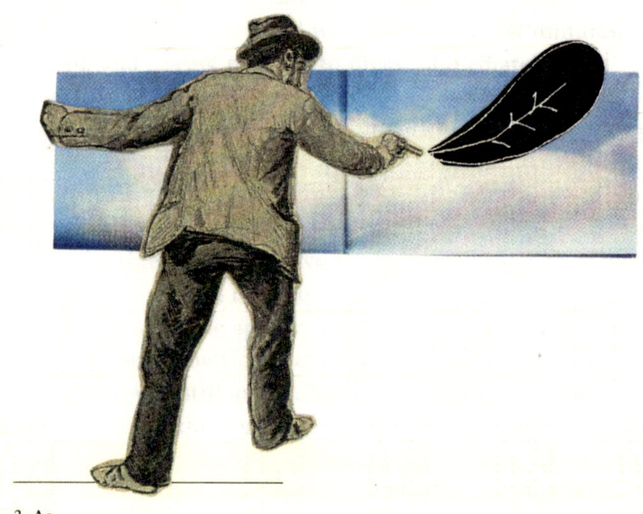

3. As

water in the bath would do

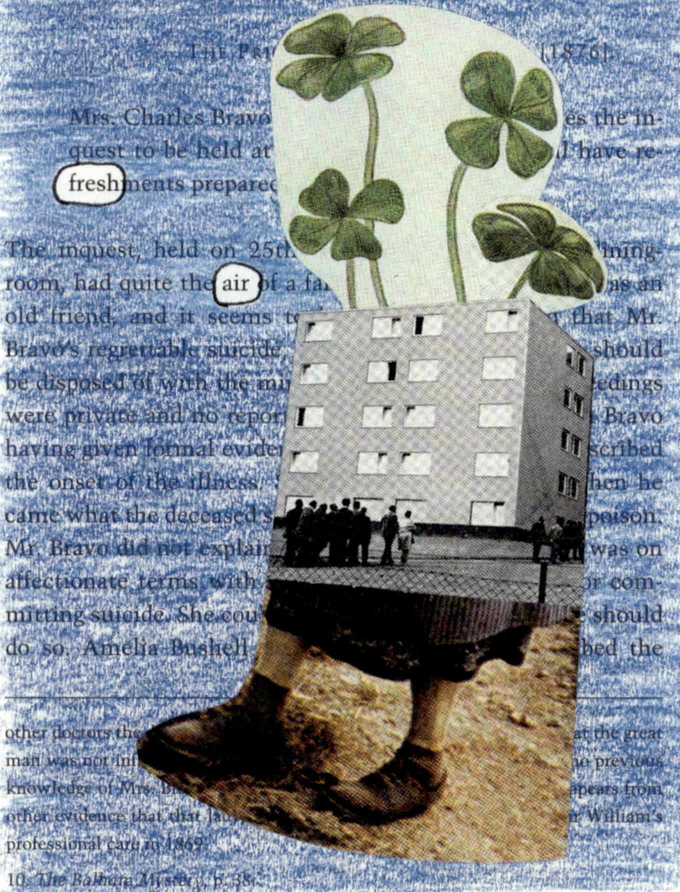
The Balham Mystery

symptoms. His last words were: "Be kind to my darling wife,
Mother, she's been the best of wives to me." The old lady's
guarded reply was, "I am never unkind to anyone."
As none of the six medical men concerned saw his way to
grant a death certificate, an inquest was inevitable, and the
Coroner's officer received in the handwriting of Mrs. Cox the
following hospitable invitation:—

THE PRI ... [1876].

Mrs. Charles Bravo ... es the in-
quest to be held at ... d have re-
freshments prepare...

The inquest, held on 25th ... dining-
room, had quite the air of a fa... as an
old friend, and it seems t... that Mr.
Bravo's regrettable suicide ... should
be disposed of with the mi... edings
were private and no report... Bravo
having given formal evide... scribed
the onset of the illness ... hen he
came what the deceased s... poison.
Mr. Bravo did not explain ... was on
affectionate terms with ... or com-
mitting suicide. She cou... should
do so. Amelia Bushell ... bed the

other doctors the... at the great
man was not inf... no previous
knowledge of Mrs. B... pears from
other evidence that that la... r William's
professional care in 1869.

10. *The Balham Mystery*, p. 38.

277

cobbling scraps of leather

in

to

dark

she-wolves

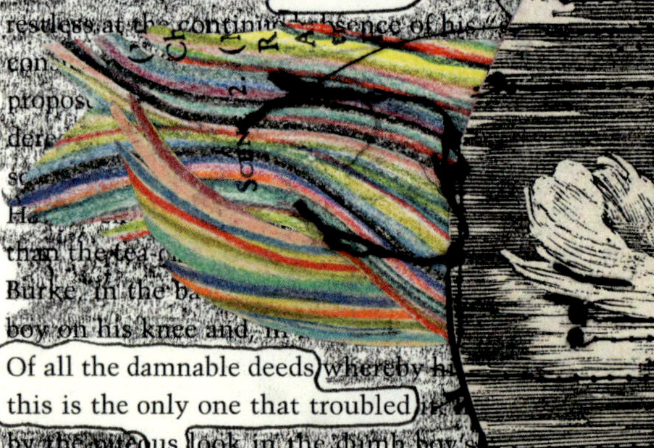

Of all the damnable deeds
this is the only one that troubled
us

with singular callousness

Four years elapsed

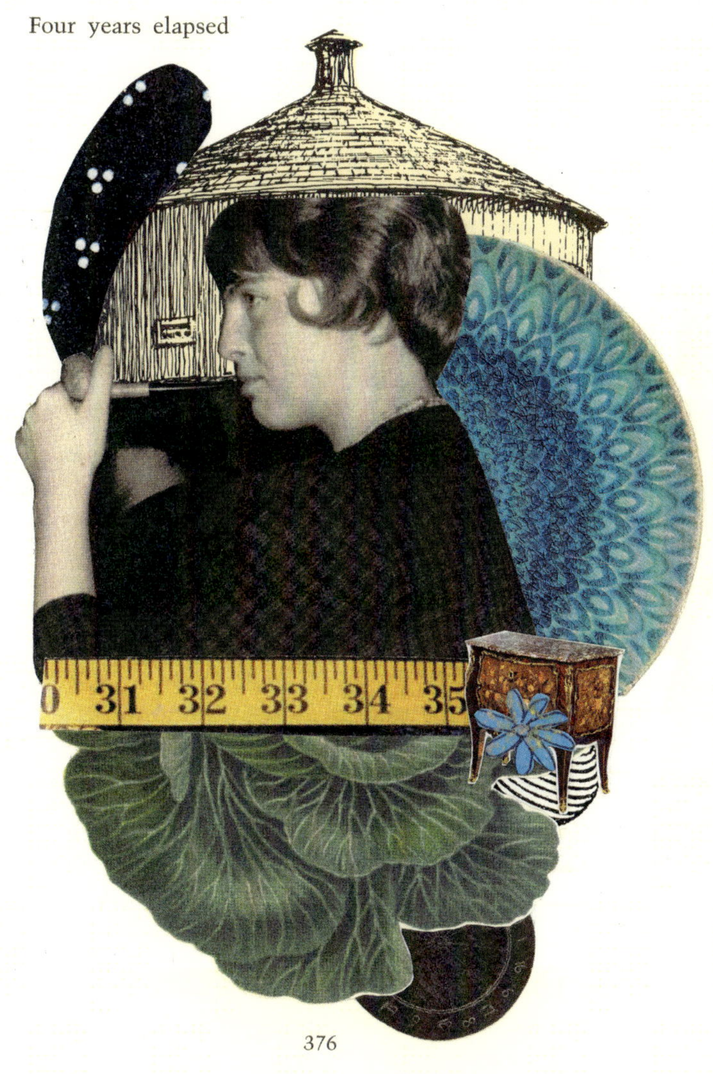

for

fiendish glee

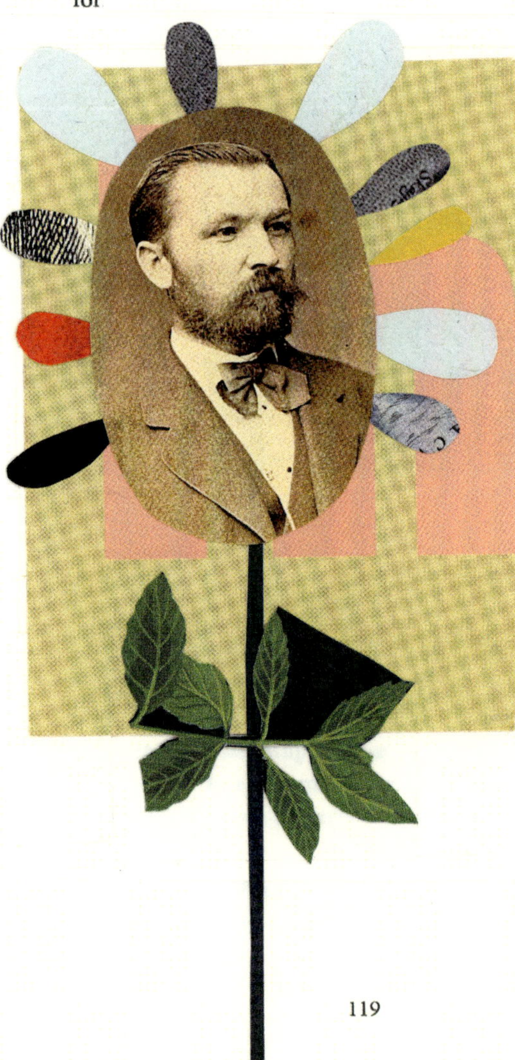

"I

ought to get

paid

119

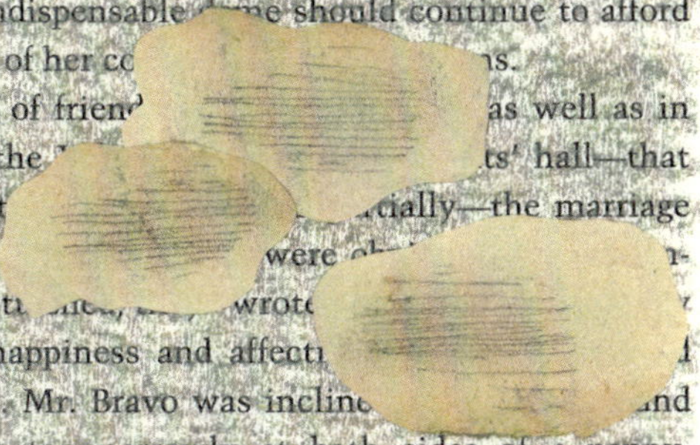

had stipulated, and Charles with a lover's complaisance had
agreed, that the indispensable […]e should continue to afford
them the comfort of her co[…]ns.

In the opinion of frien[…] as well as in
the judgment of the […]ts' hall—that
grim tribunal that […]cially—the marriage
was a success. T[…] were […]-
guage of the day, at[…] wrote […]
of their mutual happiness and affect[…]d
wholly propitious. Mr. Bravo was inclin[…]and
looked somewhat too narrowly at both sides of a penny;
but with their ample means this idiosyncrasy was negligible.
He went up to town every day, to attend the Courts or to
visit his chambers, returning at eventide to dinner; his wife,
whose domestic duties devolved upon her capable companion-
housekeeper, drove her smart pony phaeton an[…]f which
she was extremely proud, and employed the[…]sure of
a lady of that genteel period in unnecessa[…] and the
paying of perfunctory calls. But even i[…]ost placid
stream it is the practice of Fate to cas[…]sional stone:
Mrs. Bravo had a miscarriage in Januar[…]ain on 6th April
her hope of becoming a mother rece[…] a second check. She
suffered severely and made a slow recovery; it was proposed
that when she was conv[…]e should be taken for a
change to Worthing.

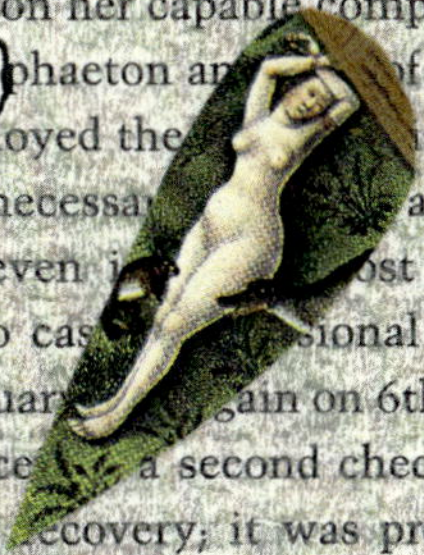

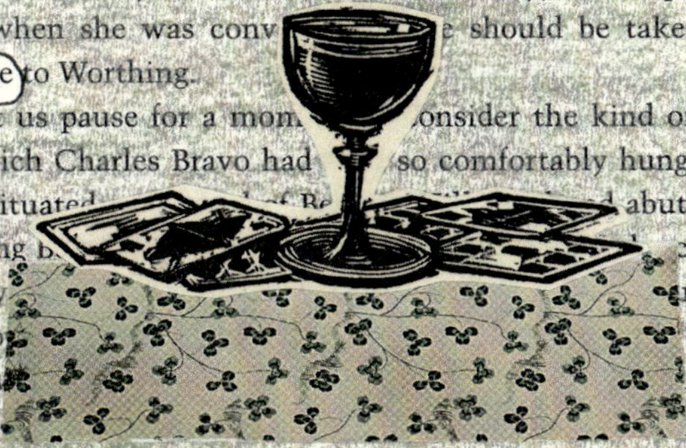

Let us pause for a mom[…]onsider the kind of house
in which Charles Bravo had […] so comfortably hung up his
hat. Situat[…] abutting on
Tooting […]contem-
porary […]rd style
of Go[…] be said
to hav[…]l." The
groun[…]rranged
and kept: there were pineries, vineries, and melon pits; and a

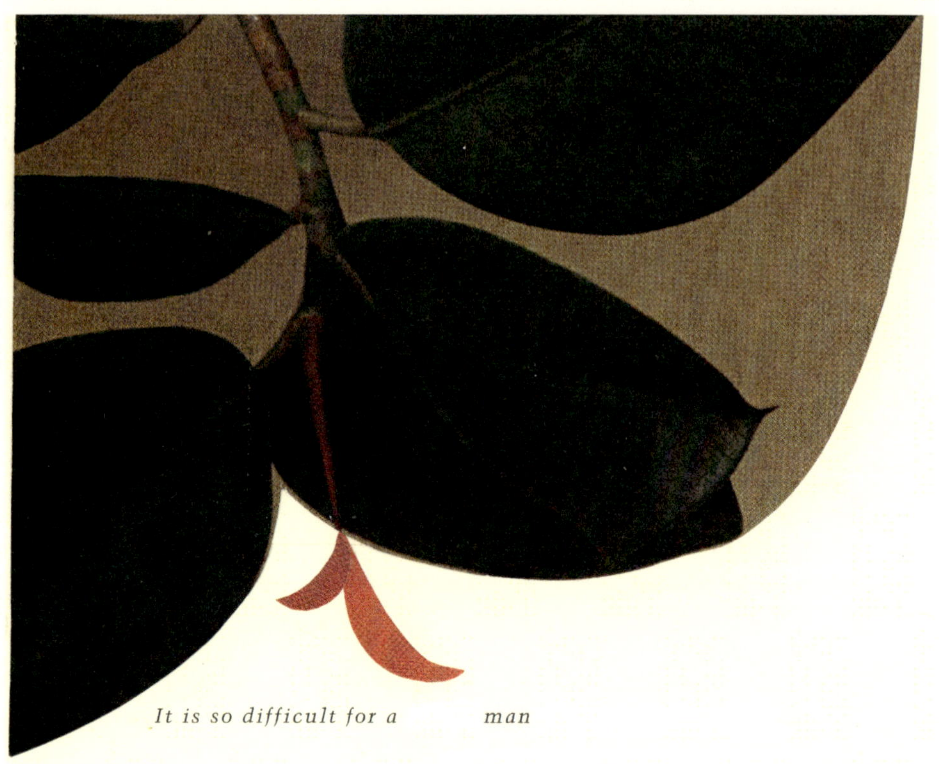

It is so difficult for a man

to
earn
an

autumn
I read in the newspapers an account

of
Such an incident
so rare as to cause
concern

379

I

went into the lobby,

as loose and hazy;

As the

the recollection of seven persons.

555

at
The séance
I
succumb to

a smile
So hard to suppress

that

in Eden
several persons
recover from their trance,

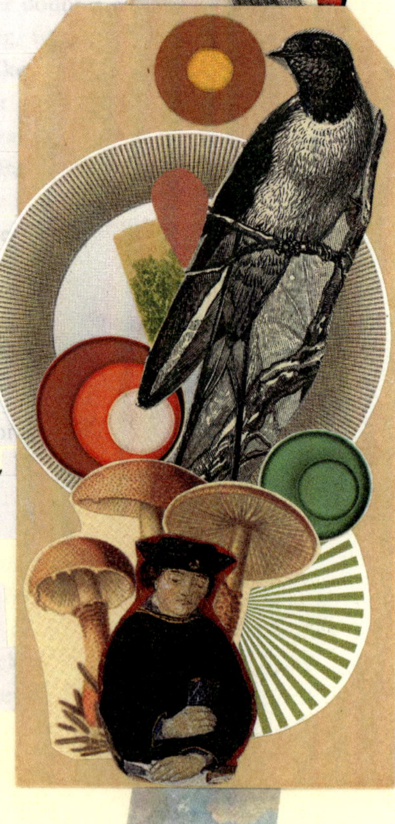

after the maids, and so on, and so forth.

morning carried
the
doom,

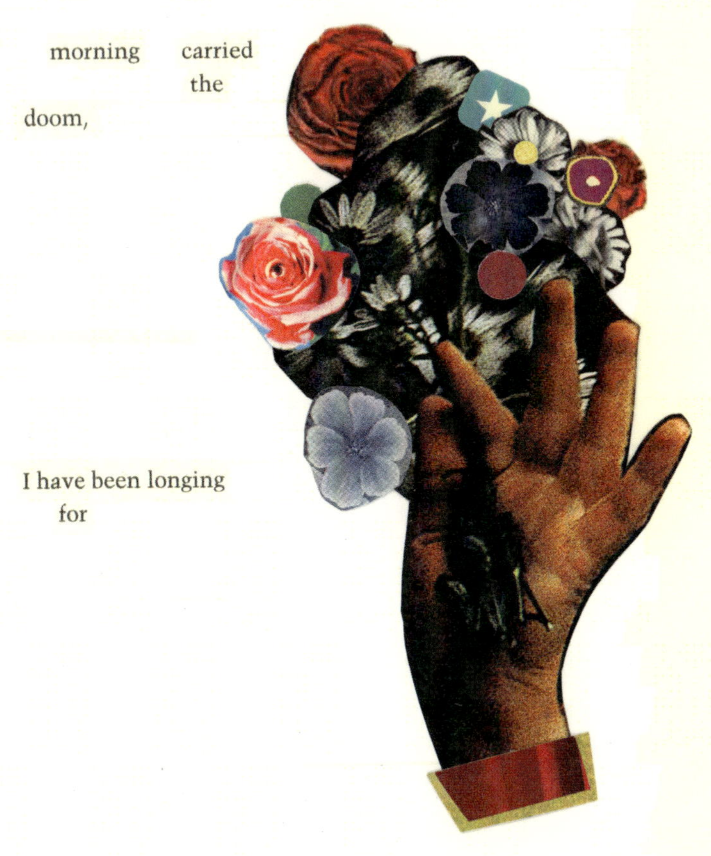

I have been longing
for

things could not remain as they were; accordingly

the Wolves of

desire

broke the long silence.

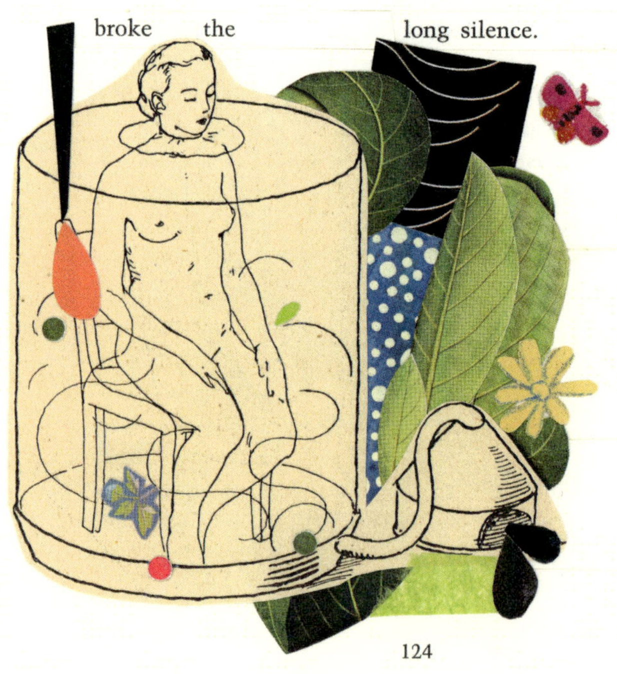

124

disinterested

was everywhere

identified

by

witnesses

was a

dense cloud

with

no address

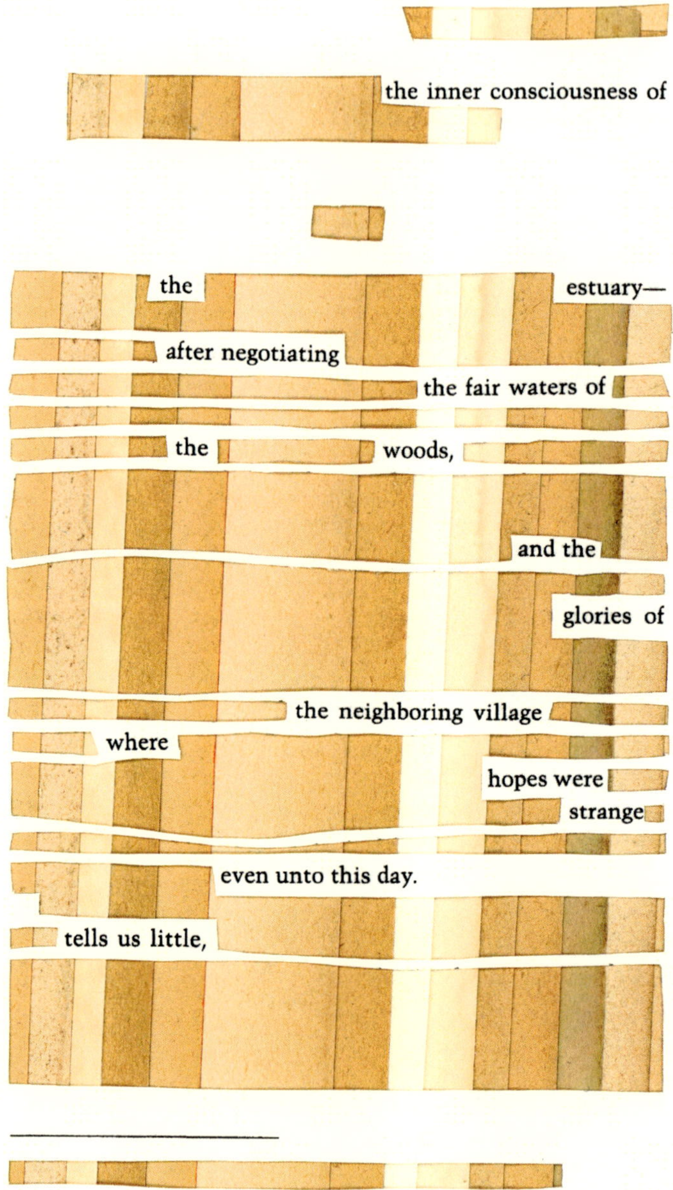

the inner consciousness of
the estuary—
after negotiating
the fair waters of
the woods,
and the
glories of
the neighboring village
where
hopes were
strange
even unto this day.
tells us little,

383

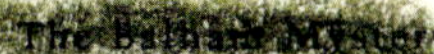

in the room, her husband often asking her to kiss him and calling her by a pet name. "What a bother I am to you all, Florrie," said he in the intervals of his pain, and he begged her to "bury him without fuss." "What have you taken, Charlie, to make you so ill?" she asked; but such was his anguish that he could only call upon his Savior for mercy.

Next day, Thursday, 20th April, the doctors informed the family that the case was hopeless and they could do no more. Mrs. Bravo then said, "You have had your way; you have given him up; now I must have my way as his wife," and she told them she had been advised—by whom, will presently appear—to try a mustard poultice, and small doses of *arsenicum*—a homeopathic drug. Dr. Johnson objected to the poultice on the ground that the patient was already sufficiently tormented, but permitted the *arsenicum,* which, Mrs. Bravo claimed, relieved the sickness. It was obtained from Mrs. Cox's medicine chest. Dr. Johnson next brought down Mr. Henry Smith, surgeon, of King's College Hospital, whose wife was a sister of Mrs. Joseph Bravo and who had known Charles from a boy. He asked the patient no questions and had nothing to suggest as to treatment.

Meanwhile Mrs. Bravo, having lost faith in the five medical experts, regardless of professional etiquette had sent Mrs. Cox to London with a note to the great Sir William Gull—who, with the unqua assistance ed five years before saved the life of the P and see if he could help her husba nothing as to circum- sta ive ce diff "Th

275

After some delay difficulty

opened

On

a

Meadow

where

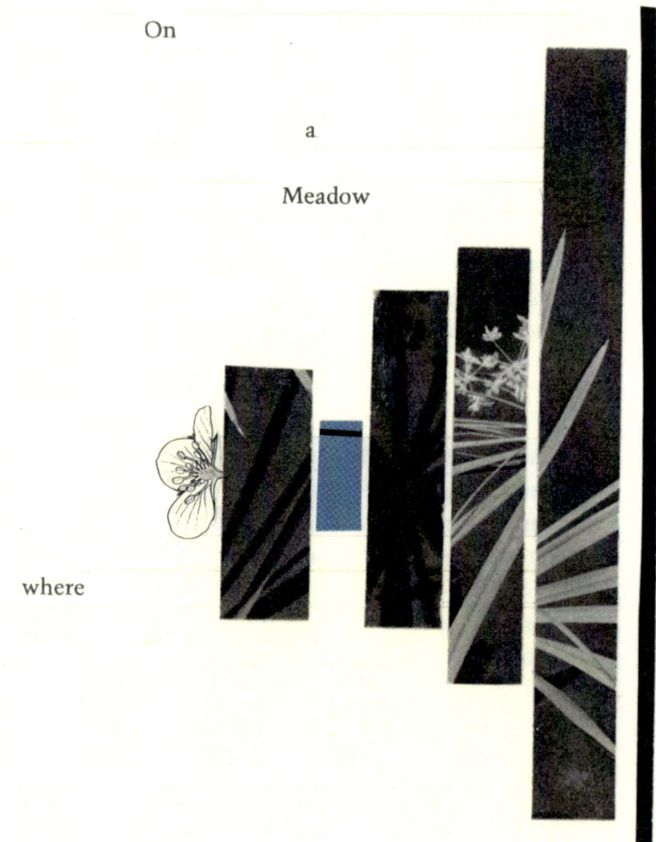

65

gloom

and cheer.

return to

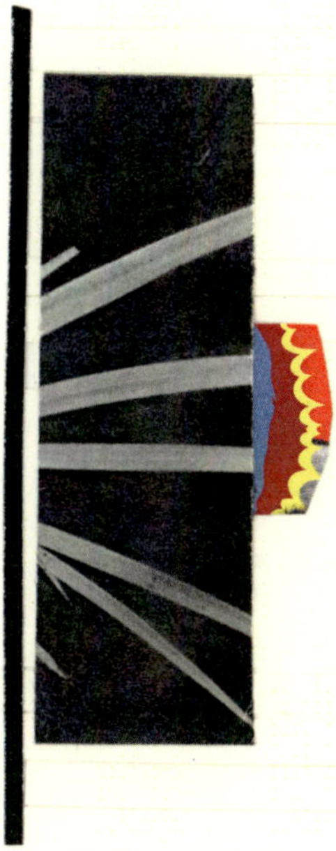

the

business

of

their own

little

explosions

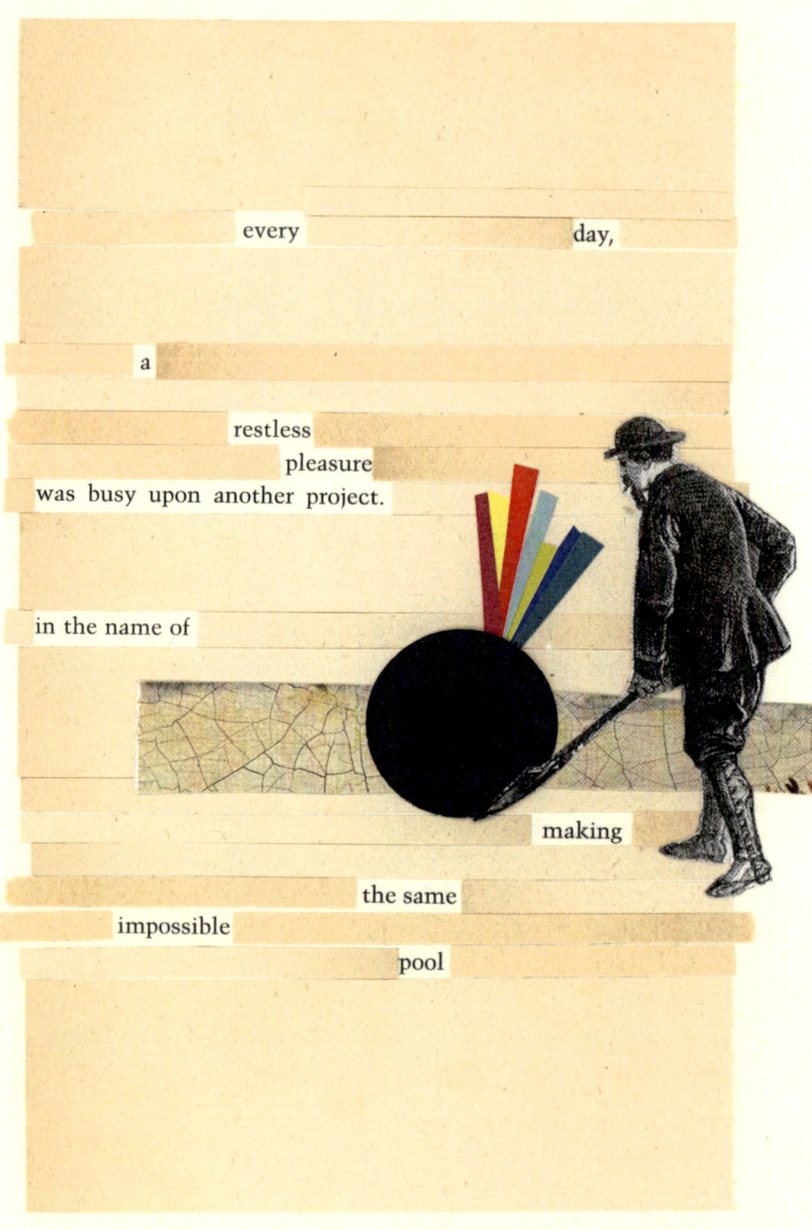
every day,
a
restless
pleasure
was busy upon another project.
in the name of
making
the same
impossible
pool

390

DRIVING UNDER THE INFLUENCE

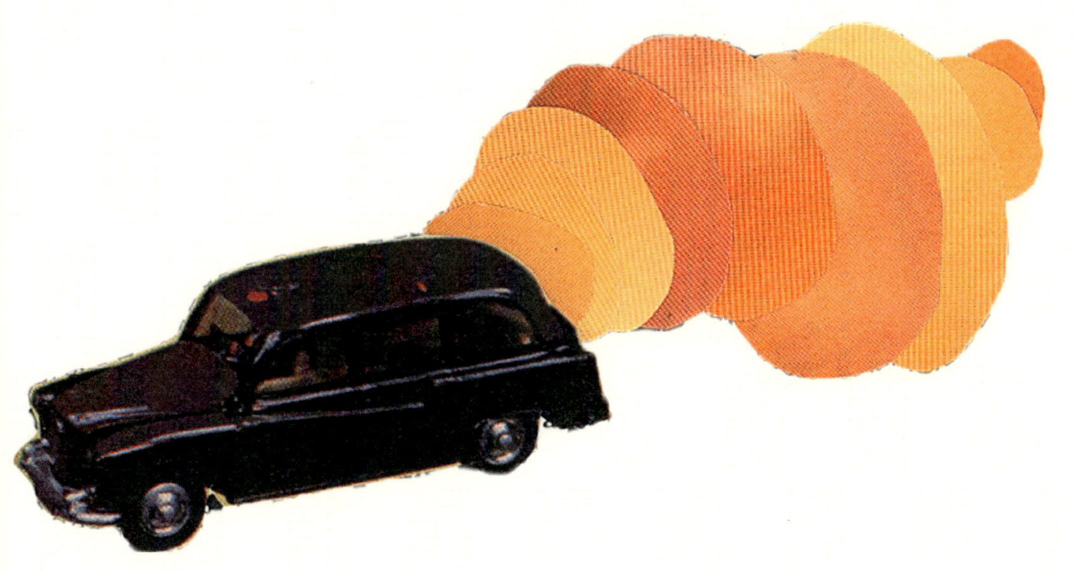

to enhance the

winter

Arrangements have been made to secure

lovable traits.

and

desert

the orthodox

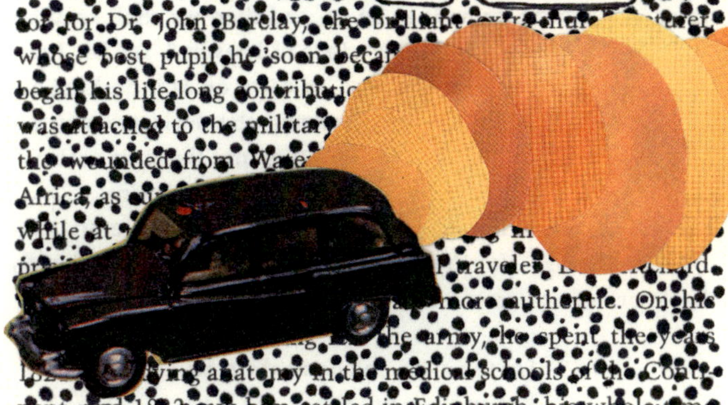

121

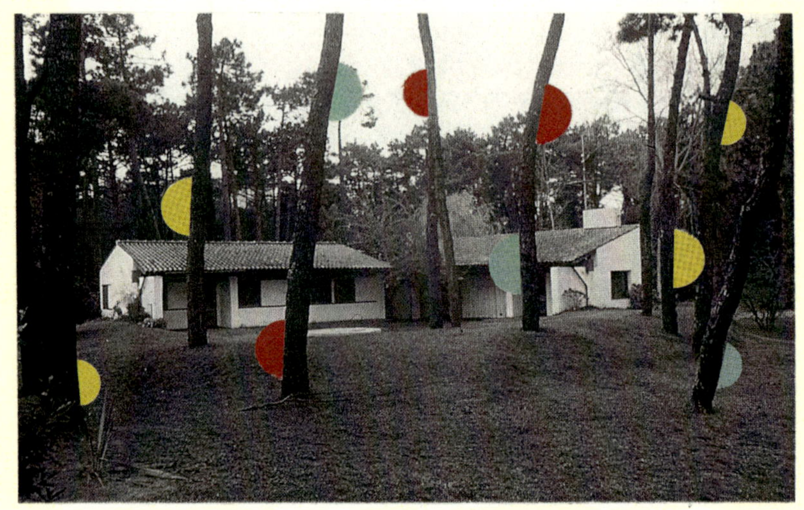

as proprietrix of
a

mean little
place of riot and revelry;
and the perpetual gurgling
heard in the land

public opinion,

was always willing to
wink at
the picturesque

95

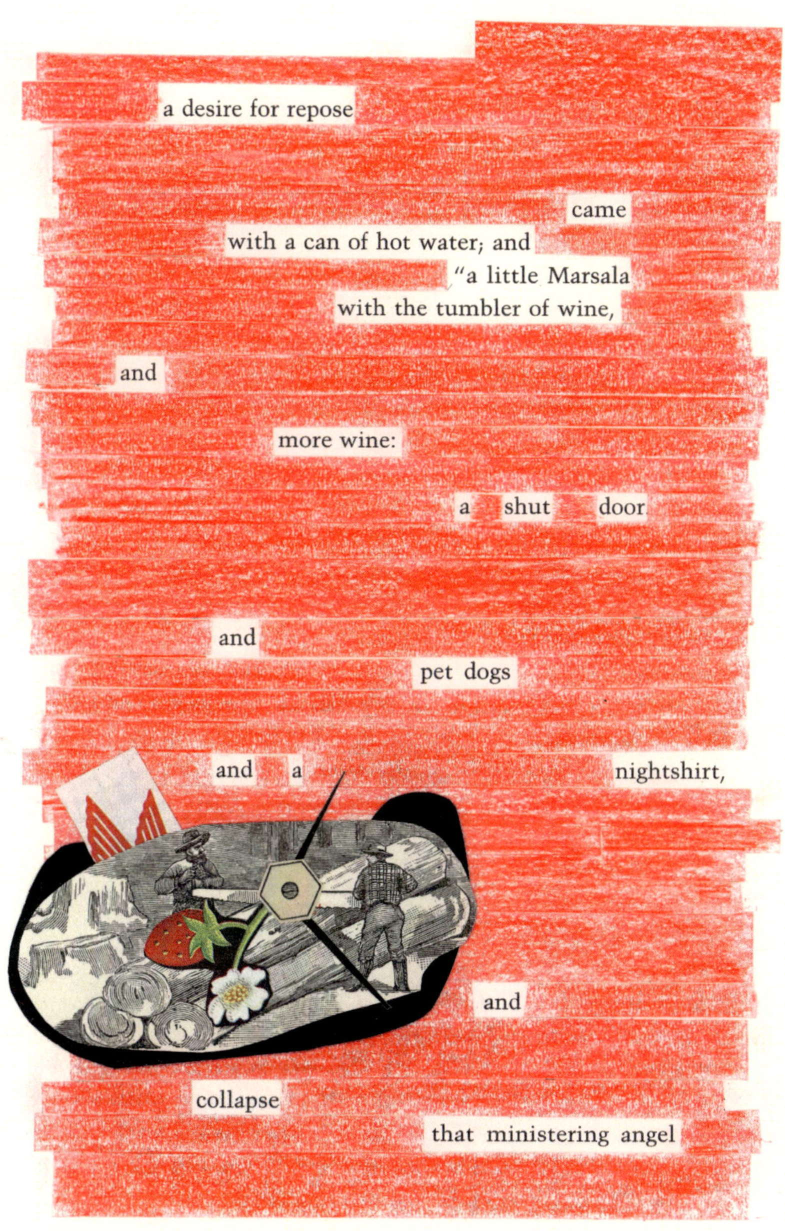
a desire for repose
came
with a can of hot water; and
"a little Marsala
with the tumbler of wine,
and
more wine:
a shut door
and
pet dogs
and a nightshirt,
and
collapse
that ministering angel

V

April is one of the

broken folk, frail,
and obscure,

my dictionary warns me

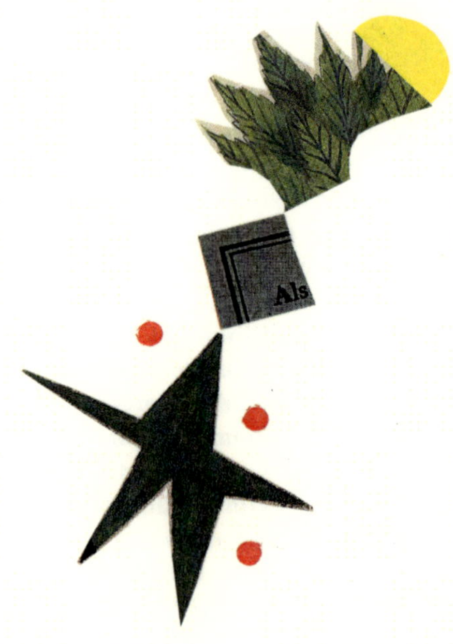

96

CLASSIC CRIMES

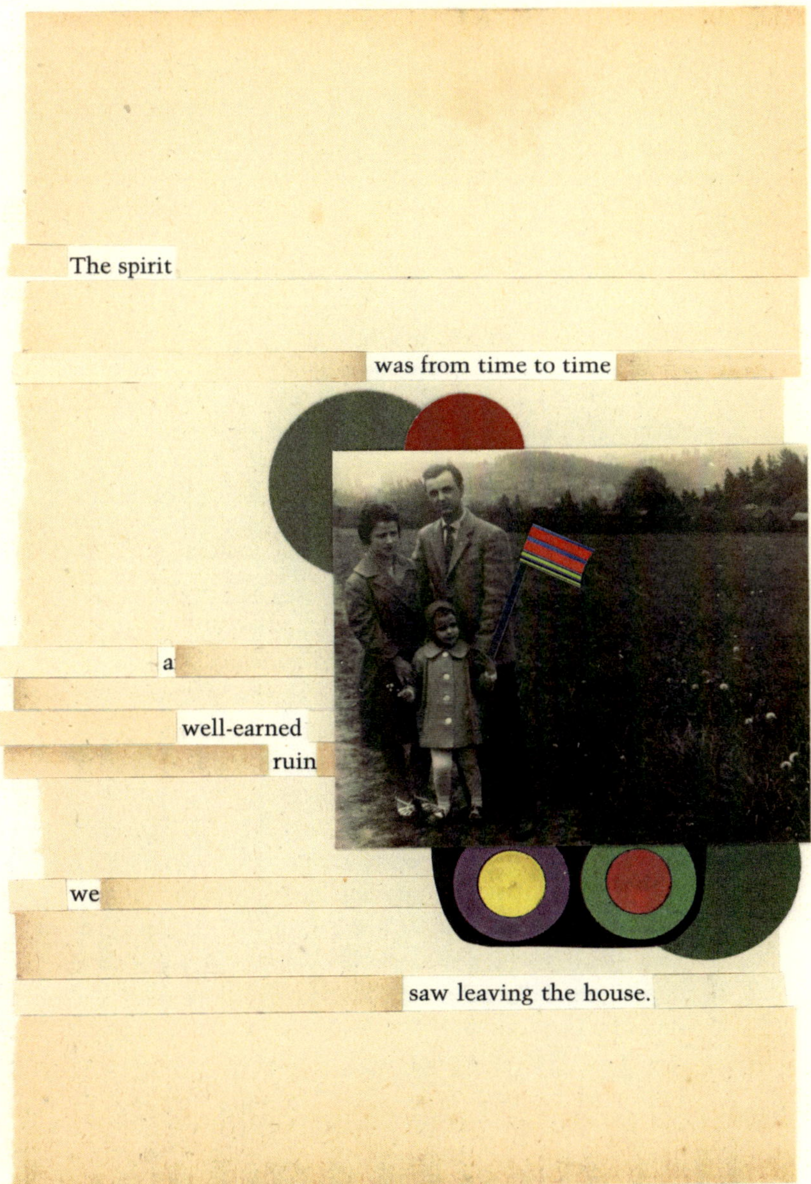

492

alighted in his usual stately fashion. He did not expect anyone to meet him, but Superintendent M'Call of the Glasgow City Police was awaiting his arrival, and at the pressing invitation of that functionary Dr. Pritchard accompanied him to the North Prison. "Previous to retiring to rest," we read, "and before the room was vacated by the officers, the Doctor engaged in prayer."[18] Doubtless he audibly petitioned for the forgiveness of his enemies, persecutors, and slanderers, and for the turning of their hearts.

The development of the case for the prosecution proceeded amain. The members of the Doctor's household were seen and precognosced, the secrets of the consulting-room laid bare,

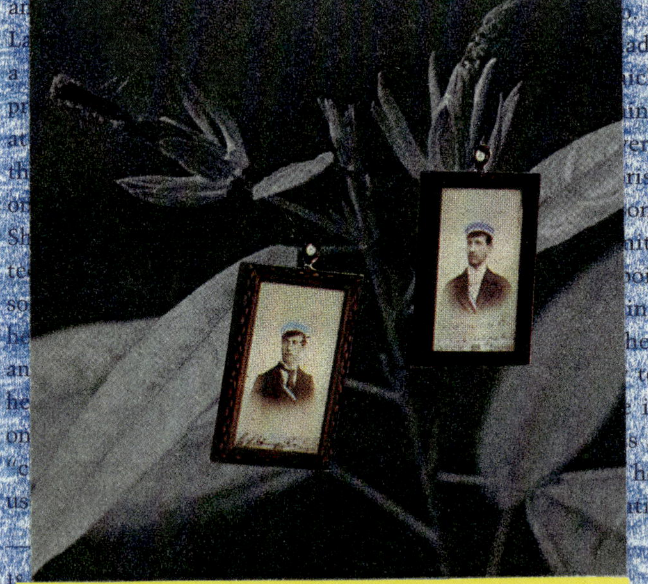

19. It is, for us, unfortunate that the autobiography … *…me Account of My Life and Writings*, Edinburgh: 1883) stops in 1862. His references to the M'Lachlan case of that year are of great interest, and one would have welcomed his reminiscences of Pritchard.

the beauty and freshness of

shock:

had

magnificent hair,

an artist

could make nothing of it.

she would ask

"How the hell can I tell about

Such a

spring

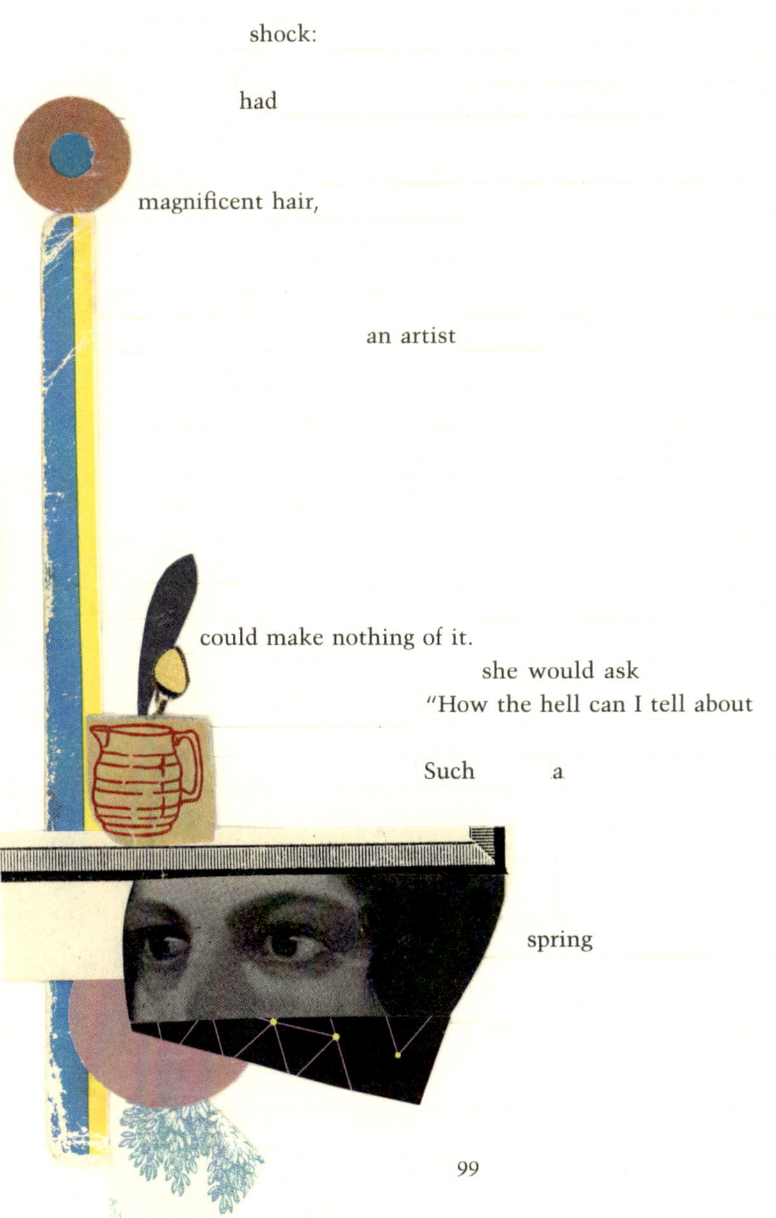

99

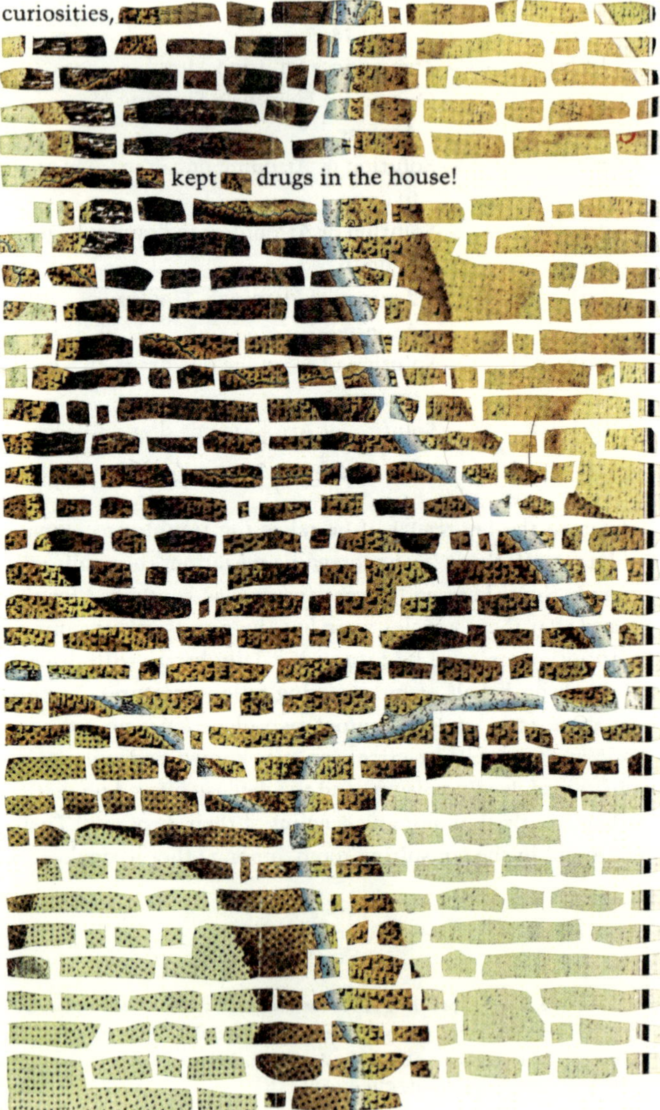

330

I

have become

a connoisseur,

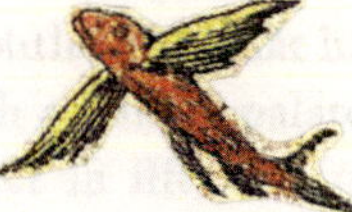

of water

held in the mouth

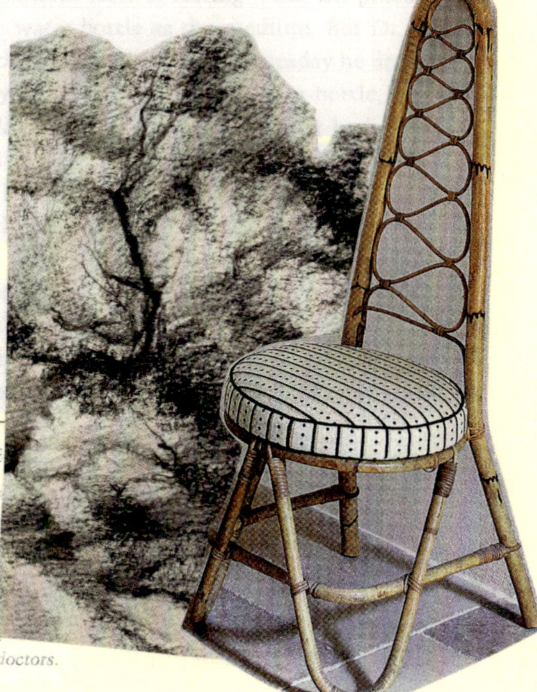

19. As to what became of

20. Why the butler (Rowe
were but one bottle, and
Moore had used some, ho
suaged his thirst? Nay, n
for camphor drops for th
ably, the bottle was em
before the arrival of the doctors.

the tragedy

is

When

you worry

About noon
it being

small

careful,

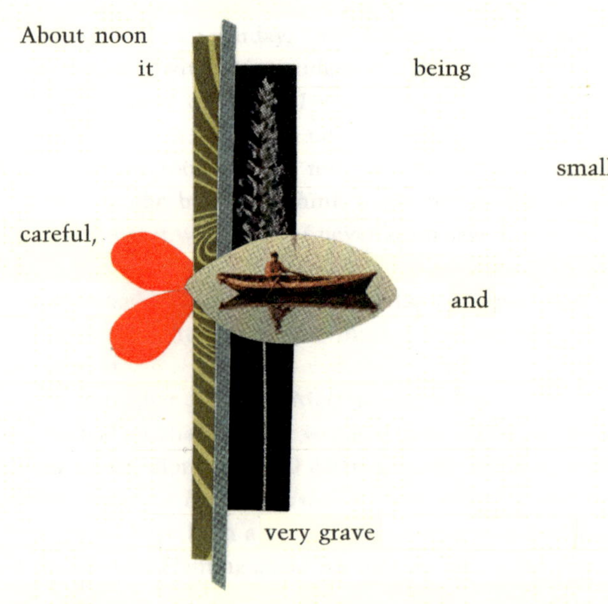

and

very grave

533

night
garbed in
gaudy hues
was
hanged upon a tree in the
garden
and
persuaded at length
to retire from the field

123

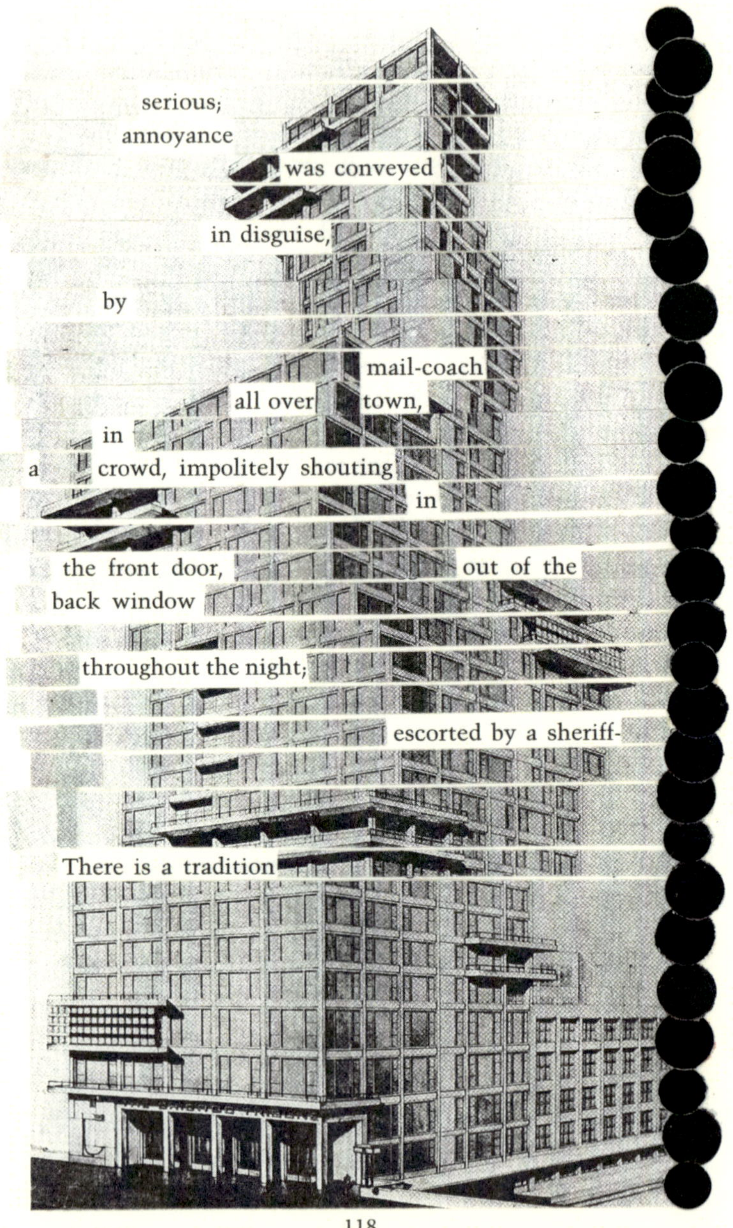

serious;
annoyance
was conveyed
in disguise,
by
mail-coach
all over town,
in
a crowd, impolitely shouting
in
the front door, out of the
back window
throughout the night;
escorted by a sheriff-
There is a tradition

118

delicate

MANSIONS,

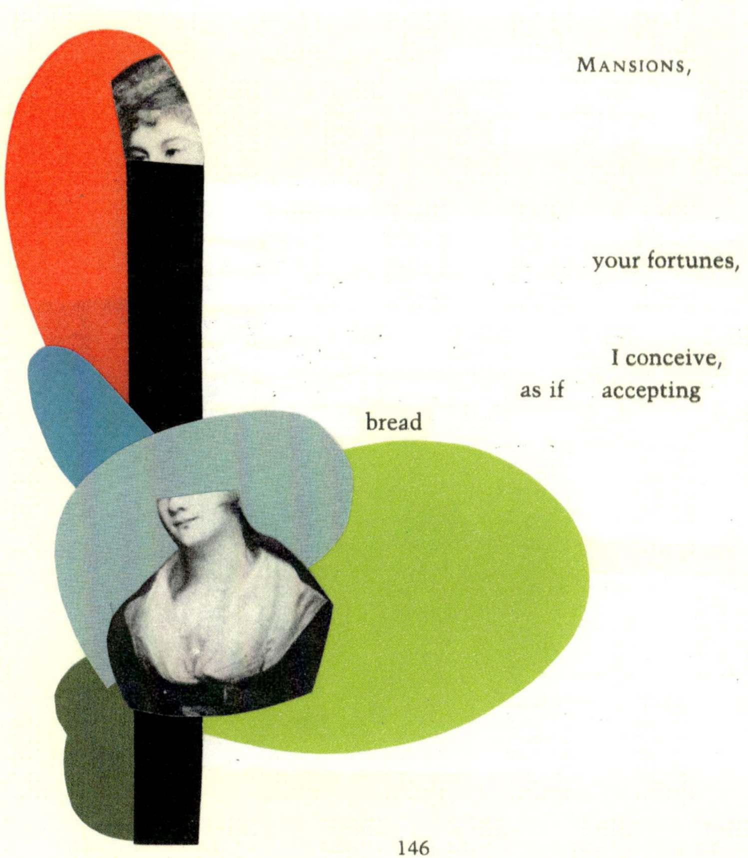

your fortunes,

I conceive,
as if accepting
bread

146

downstairs herself, and ordered the butler to send the coachman for Dr. Harrison of Streatham Hill—instead, as one should have expected from one of her capacity, for the nearest doctor.

Meanwhile Mary Ann had wakened Mrs. Bravo, and told her that Mr. Bravo was very ill. Twice crying, "What is the matter?" the wife threw on her dressing-gown and hastened to her husband's assistance. She was horrified to find him lying insensible on the floor by the window: "he was looking like death." The moment she heard that Dr. Harrison had been summoned from Streatham, she said to Mrs. Cox, "Why didn't you send for Dr. Moore?" who lived hard by. Running downstairs, she met the butler as he returned from his message to the lodge. She was crying, he says, and seemed sincerely anxious. She bade him fetch Dr. Moore forthwith, which he did. When Dr. Moore came shortly after ten he found the two ladies with the patient, who had been lifted into a chair; he was totally unconscious, the pulse barely perceptible. "He looked like a person who was under the influence of poison," but what poison, the doctor failed to ascertain. He was put to bed, and Mrs. Bravo asked whether his condition was dangerous; being told to expect the worst, she burst into tears, her grief appearing to Dr. Moore to be perfectly genuine. Some half-hour later Dr. Harrison arrived. He was met at the door by Mrs. Cox, who was more communicative to him than to his confrère; she informed him of vomiting at the window and of the admi ion of the rd emet ding: *"I am sure he has t chloroform."* After consulting h Dr. Moore, Dr. Harri collapse and quit andy. In

the gowns
lie till called for.
and
all this

time
in the
[dressing] room

a
syllable of
want

is
listened to

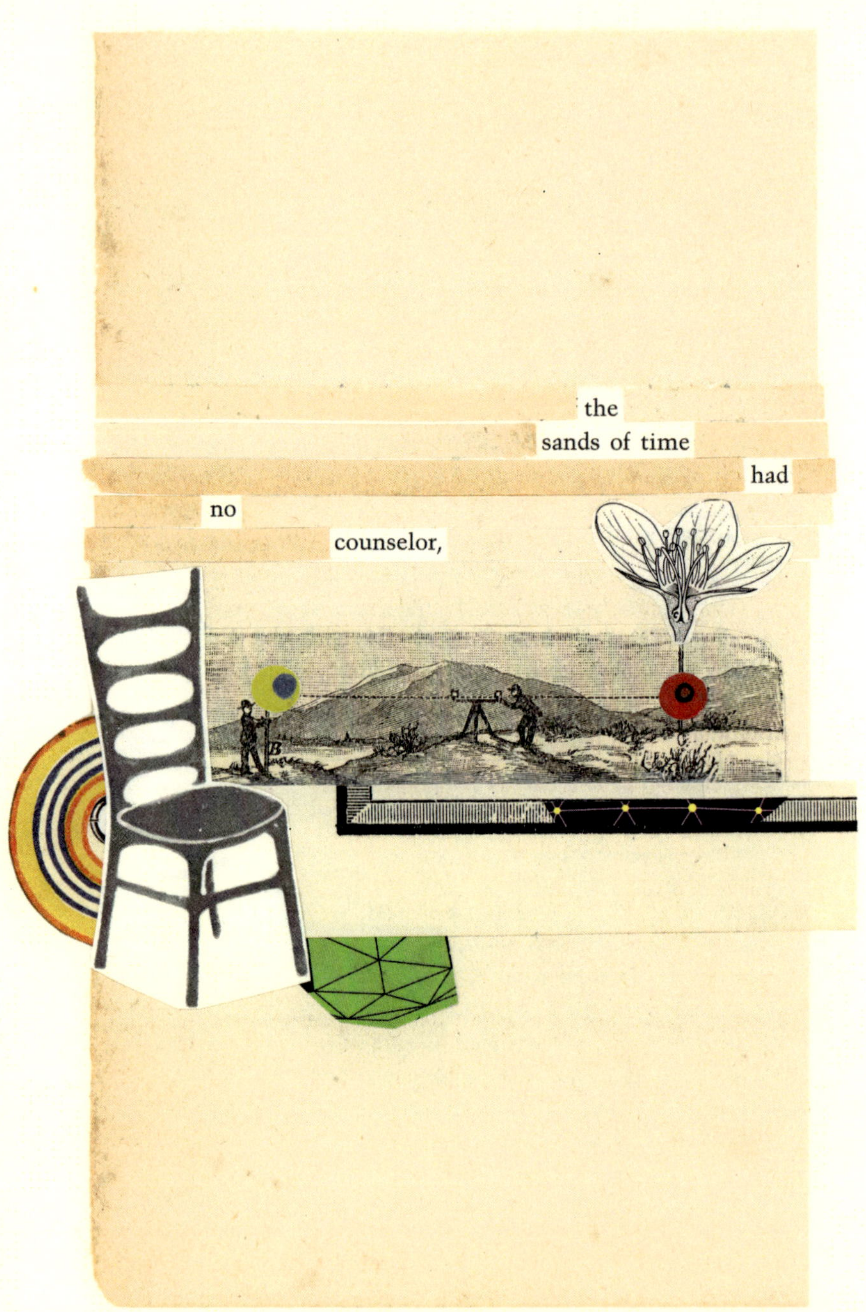

119

has never alluded to the matter [of the r der] to me since it occurred, from first to last. The young es have and so has Miss Const , and Master William has often cried over it.

The thiro 's hearing began with the evidence of M ter William, who had nothing to tell, and of other witnesses, who were in the same situation. Then Mr. Parsons, the surgeon, gave an elab e account of the nortem, at which it now appeared that Stapleton, the orian of the case, assisted. He was more positive about the appearance of the mouth: "It had been pressed for a considerable time—say, m five to ten minutes, and by a soft substance."[14] His final nion was that the child d from suffocation, and that the several injuries were inflicted *after* death. The remainder of the tting was occupied by witnesses of no importance. Mrs. Dall ore, wife of a Trowbridge constable, who seems een placed by Foley as a spy upon the n , gave an livers conversations had with her, as ll before apprehension. Gough, however, while maintaini nocence, had steadily refused to inculpate a anifest annoy of the police woman.[15] t the "chest flannel" found in the f all the female inmates, but den well. She was much disc

The fourth and last d to Mr. Ribton's long and ent hich I have no space to er. He conte owed

14. Mr. Stapleton was of opinion that th hysio- logically to decapitation. It would at on all re- sistanc he murderous cut had drain conds of their ; but that from the small luced the distention and suffusion of the face, uffo- cation.—*The Great Crime of 1860*, p. 62.

ress the opinion that th was to "jealousy," and she may well have had her own

significance

was employed as
a good voice,
in the choir,

of

dense sea fog;

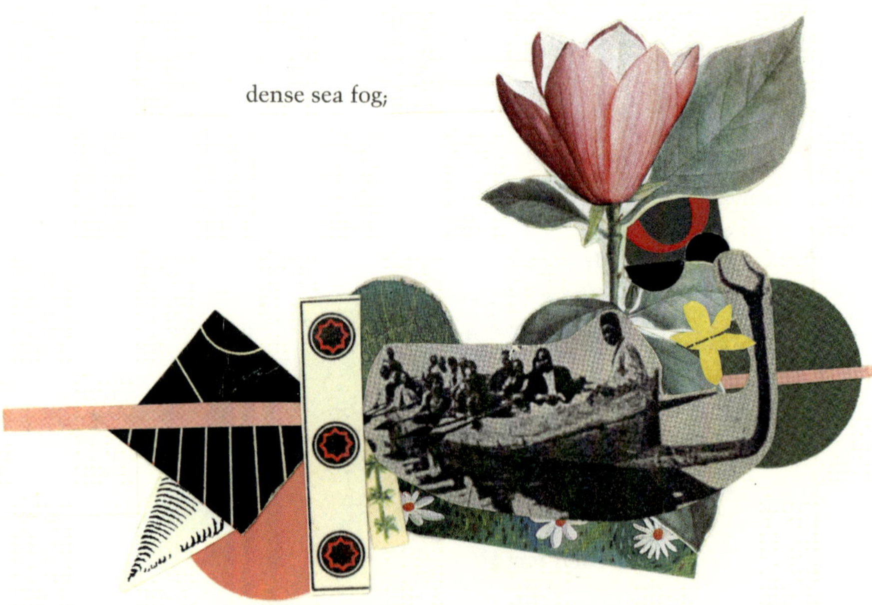

376

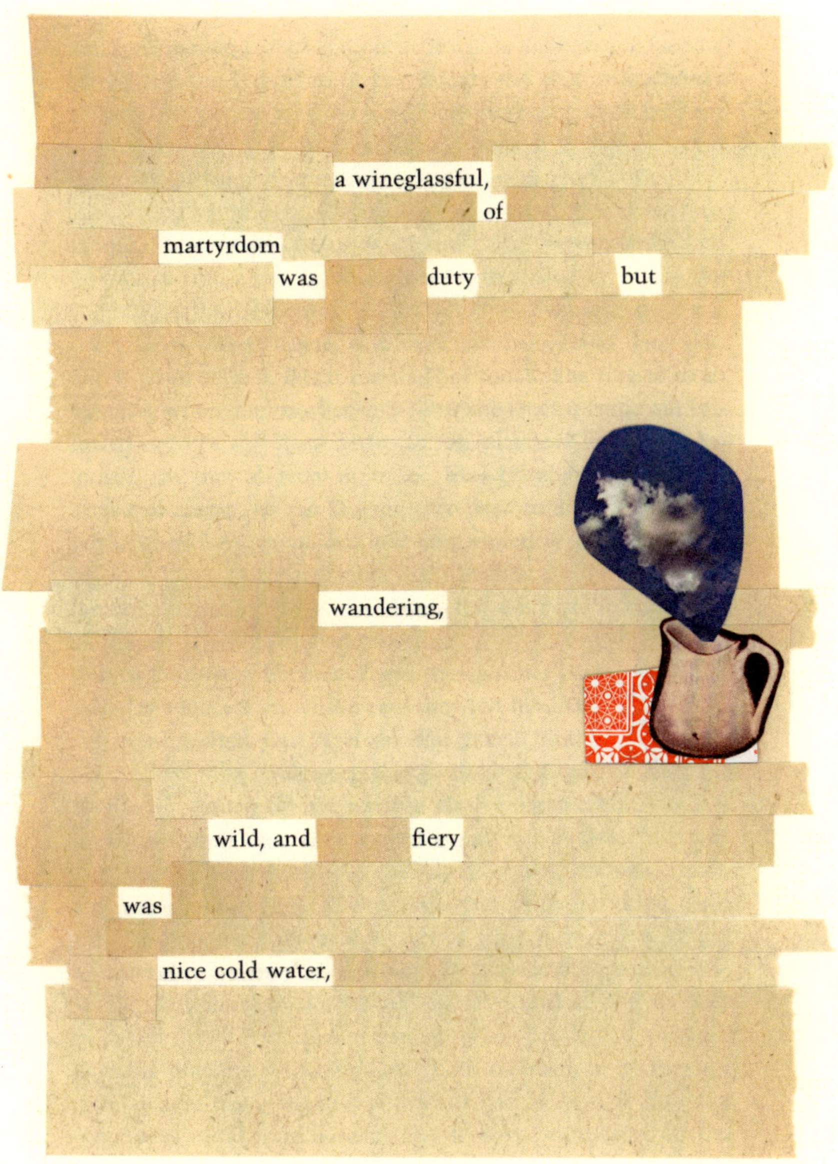
a wineglassful,
of
martyrdom
was duty but
wandering,
wild, and fiery
was
nice cold water,

money for her own expenses. "You know my little purse?" said she; "there are £6 in it, take what you want to go on with."

Now Mrs. Hill, although she did not tell her friend, had to return to London that night, and wished to hear more of the matter from Merrett before she did so. He had promised to come back for her at lunch-time, but failed to appear; she waited some hours in vain and then returned to the hotel, whence she rang up the Infirmary at intervals without getting hold of him. Sister Grant referred her to his spiritual home, the Dunedin Palais de Danse, where she was equally unsuccessful. Mrs. Hill then telegraphed to her friend's sister, Mrs. Penn, who with her husband was on the Riviera. They at once set out for Scotland, and in London heard from Mrs. Hill on her return so much as she knew of the mystery of Mrs. Merrett's injury and illness.

The Penns reached Edinburgh on the morning
exactly a week after the shooting. Mrs. Merrett w
sister with joy. She asked Mrs. Penn to get her an e
the Infirmary people said she had had a fall, but
lieve it. "She said she was sitting at the table
sudden explosion went off in her head"—to
arresting words: "as if Donald had shot m
that of course that was impossible. Mrs.
to get a present for Sister Grant, who h
to go to the flat for her fur coat, to liv
look after Donald," etc., all which M

Next day, the 25th, Mrs. Merret
for £5 for Mrs. Hill's expenses, bei
end—her left side was paralyzed as
that night she became delirious,
27th, unconscious, in which state
early in the morning of Thursda
the infliction of her wound. The c
basal meningitis, following a bull

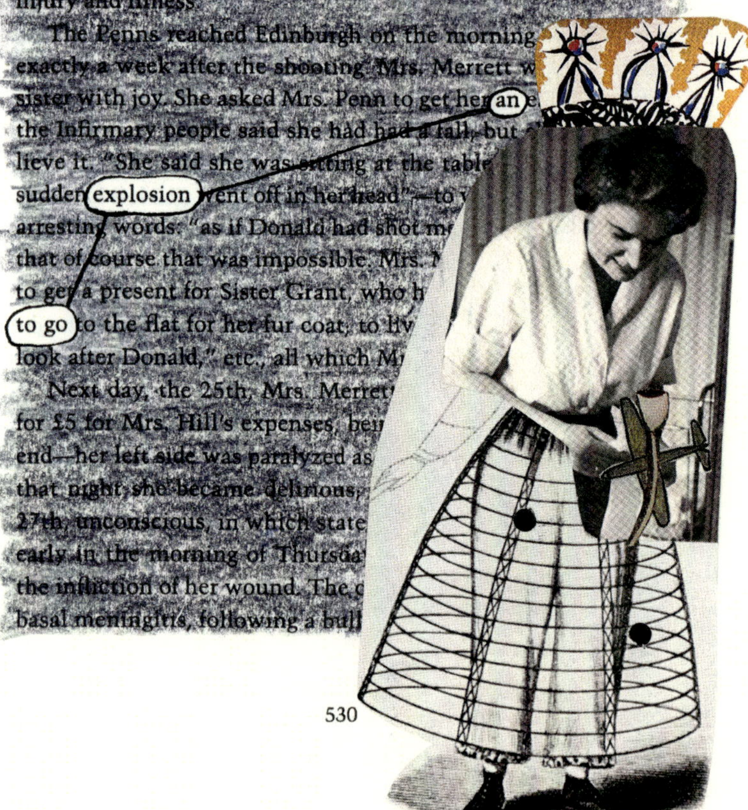

530

DISTURBING THE PEACE

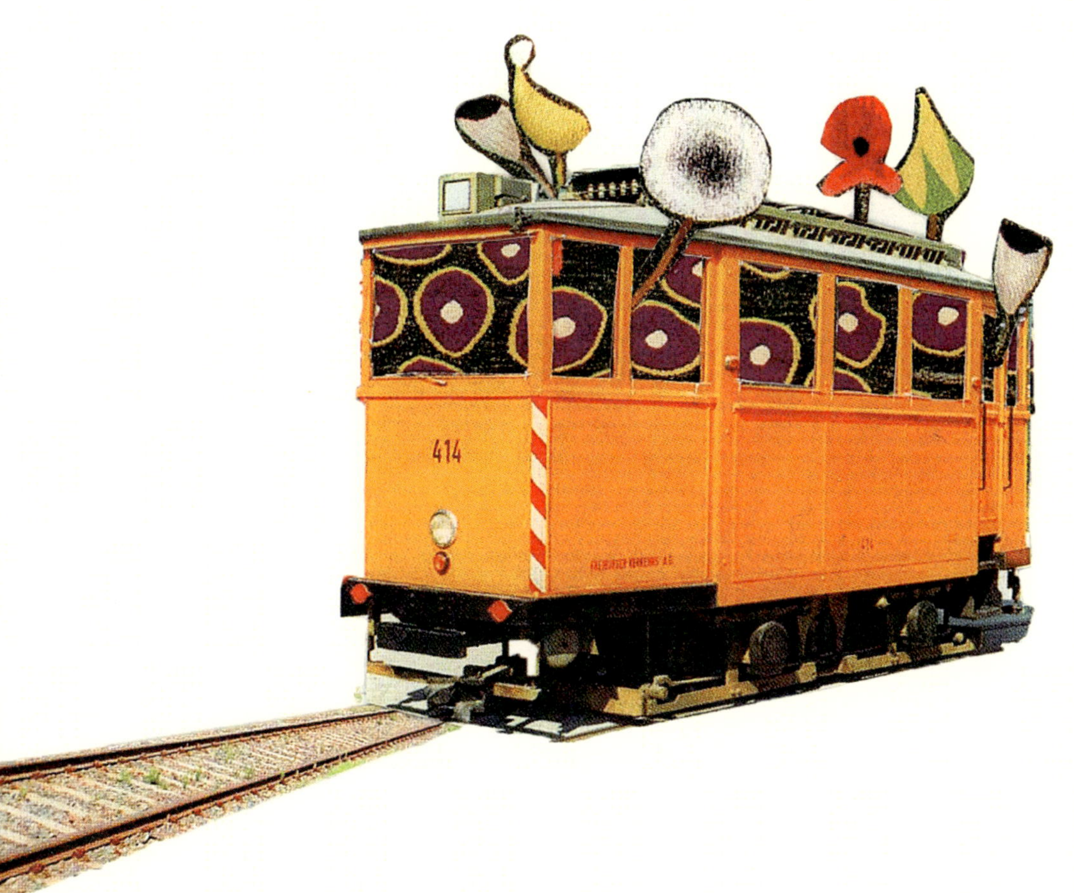

reading, and I do not propose to dwell on it. His once crowded classes gradually dwindled. "His star was on the ebb," Dr. Lonsdale sadly records, "and the growing animosity of his contemporaries rendered the ebb more and more apparent." In 1837 he applied for the Chair of Pathology, vacant by the resignation of Dr. John Thomson, whom, having declined professional preferment, Dr. Knox in his flippant way called "the old chair-maker." He was not appointed, and in a later application for the Chair of Physiology he was also unsuccessful. In 1839 he gave up his old rooms in Surgeons' Square to become a lecturer on anatomy in the Argyle Square Medical School—a marked declension. His next move was to Glasgow, where he tried to establish himself again as a teacher, but the enrolments for his class were so few that he returned the fees. In London, his final resort, he was for a time, according to his biographer, in general practice at Hackney; and "one of his last occupations," Sir Robert Christison tells us, "was that of lecturer, demonstrator, or showman, to a traveling party of Ojibbeway Indians." He died on 20th December 1862 at the age of 71, and was buried at Woking. Recalling their relative positions, his fate was as terrible as that of Hare and less merciful than Burke's.

■

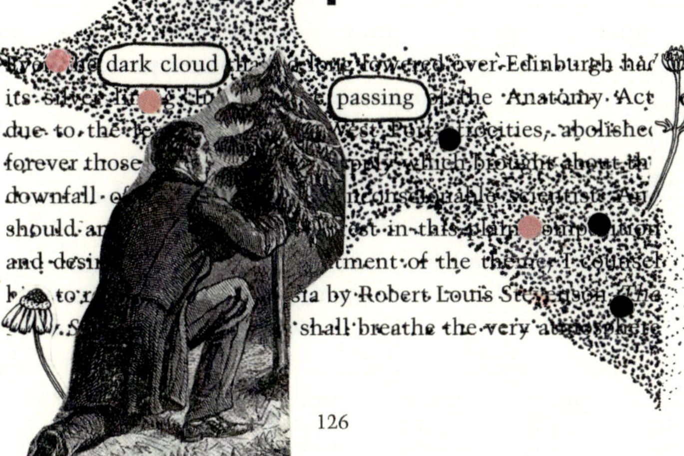

... dark cloud ... lowered over Edinburgh had its silver lining ... passing of the Anatomy Act due to the ... West Port atrocities, abolished forever those ... which brought about the downfall of ... scientists ... should ... in this ... and desire ... sentiment of the theme I counsel him to ... by Robert Louis Stevenson ... shall breathe the very atmosphere

o

omens

at eventide in

the aimless leisure

that

is

suffered severely

Let us pause

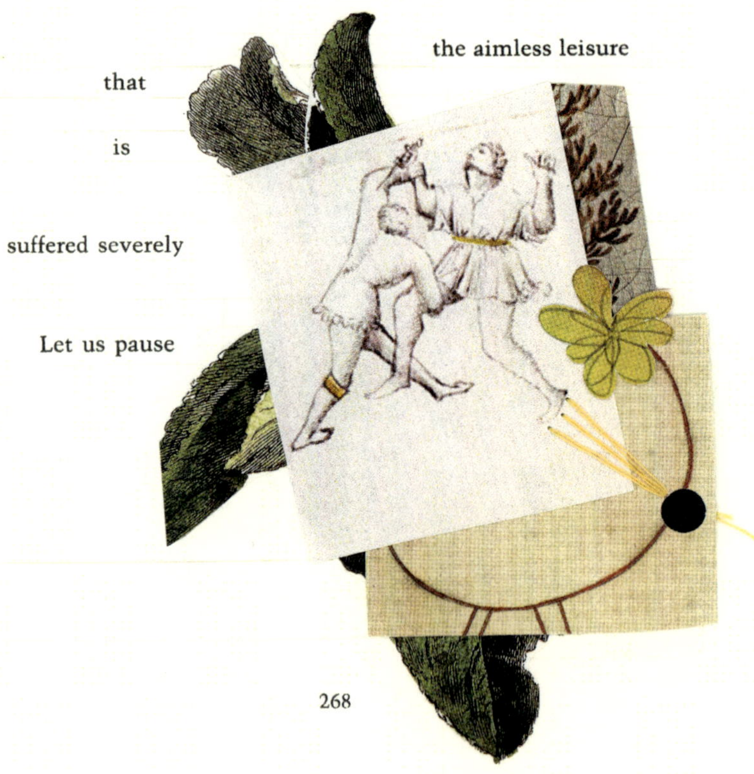

268

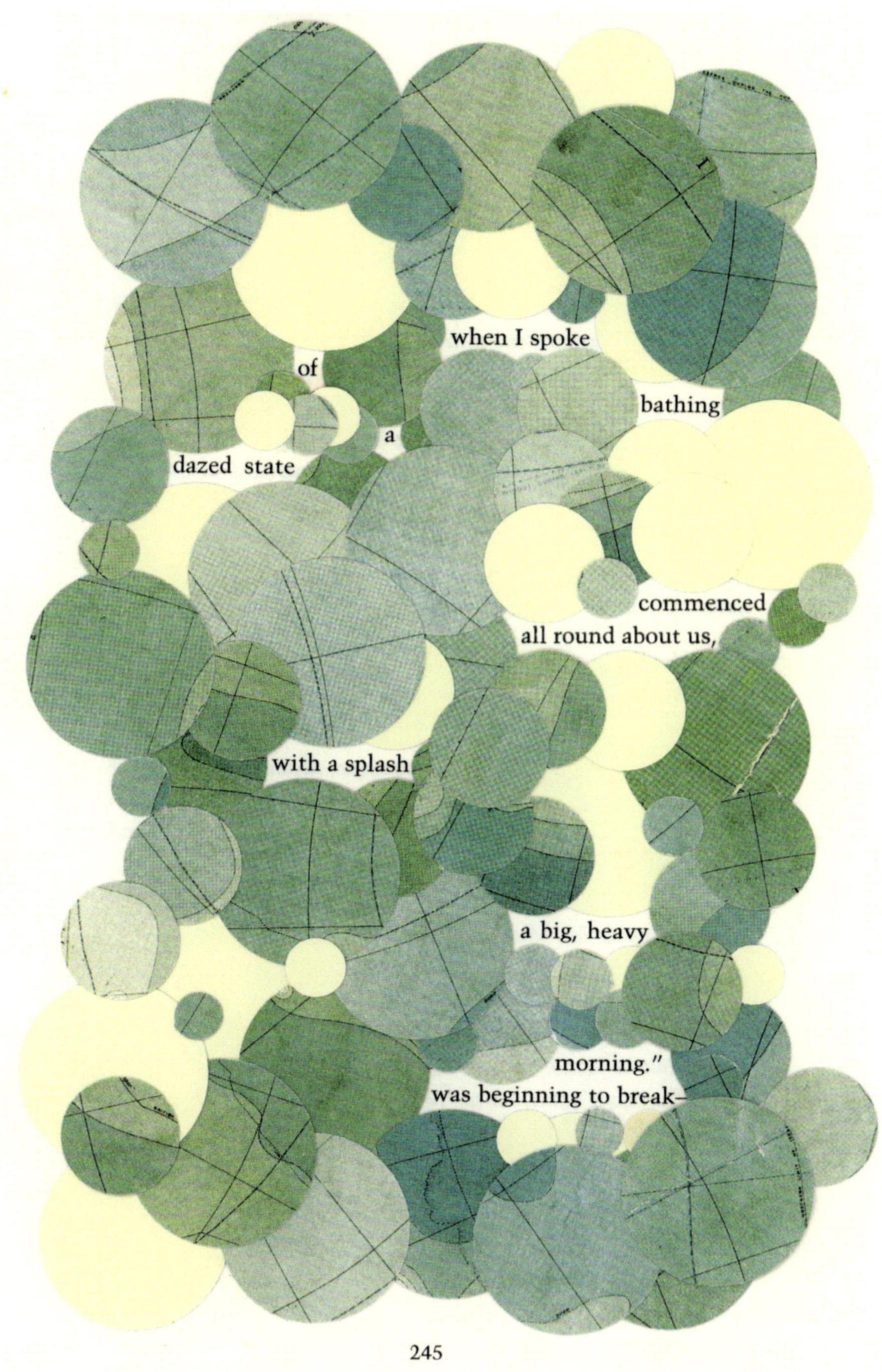
when I spoke
of
bathing
a
dazed state
commenced
all round about us,
with a splash
a big, heavy
morning."
was beginning to break-
245

6 Windsor Place, 4th March 1865.

Dear Sir,—I am surprised that I am called to
this
short
narcotic,
moment
which is

sudden, and to me mysterious.—

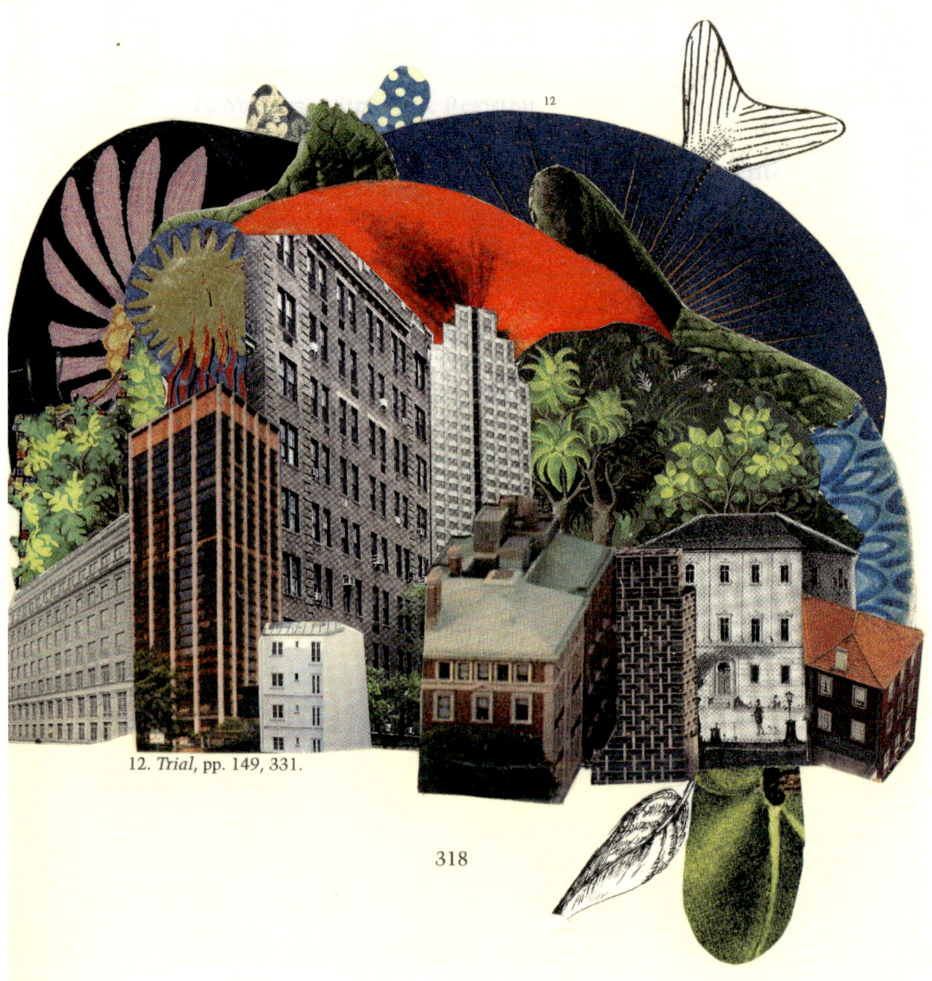

12. *Trial*, pp. 149, 331.

to

sleep says authority,

is

an interlude

of

little dinners

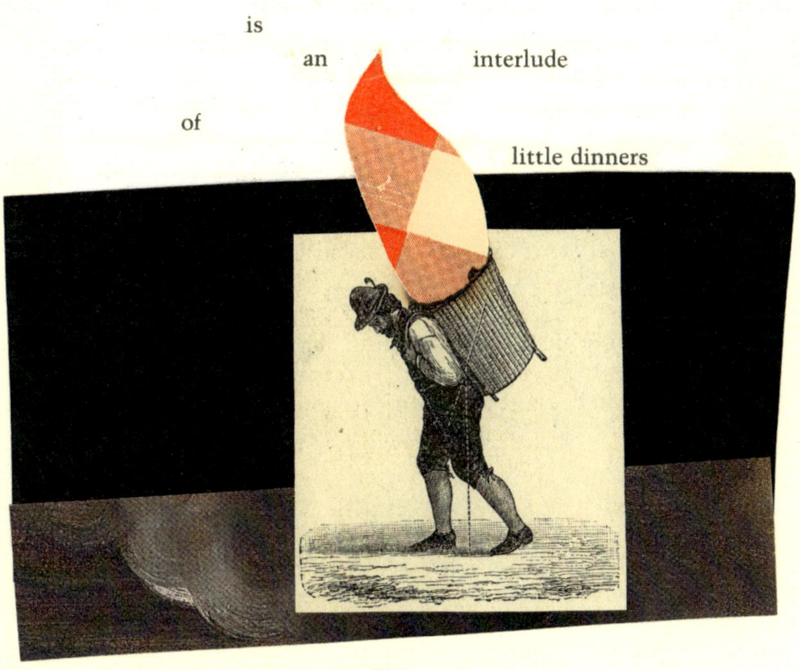

385

7

---

7. Strangely enough,

the ring of truth.[8]

8. *Mystery,*

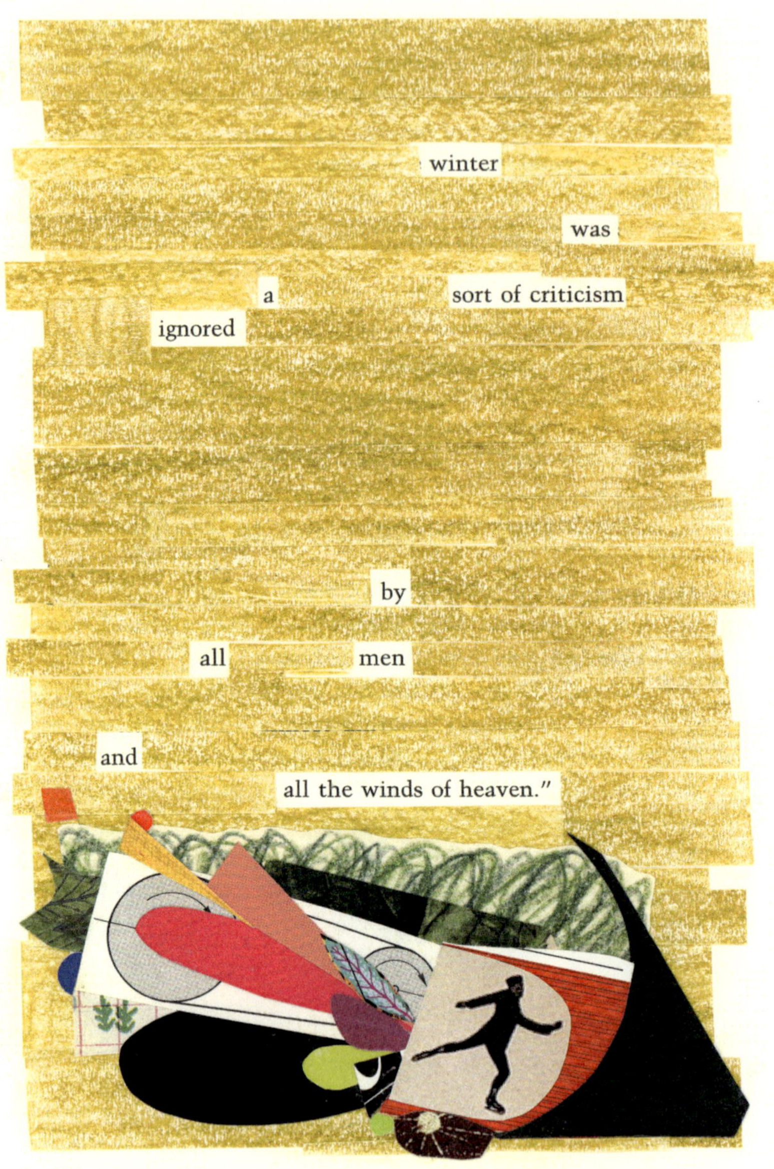
winter
was
a
sort of criticism
ignored
by
all
men
and
all the winds of heaven."

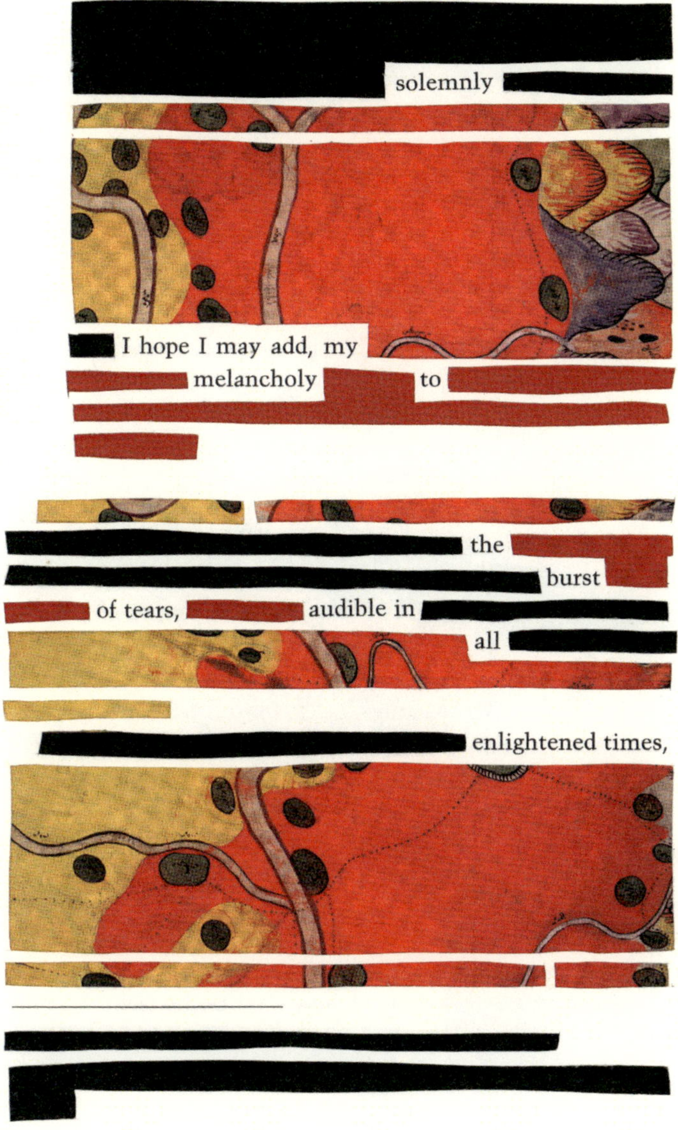
solemnly
I hope I may add, my
melancholy to
the
burst
of tears, audible in
all
enlightened times,

—I would give so much

To

rest my telescope on

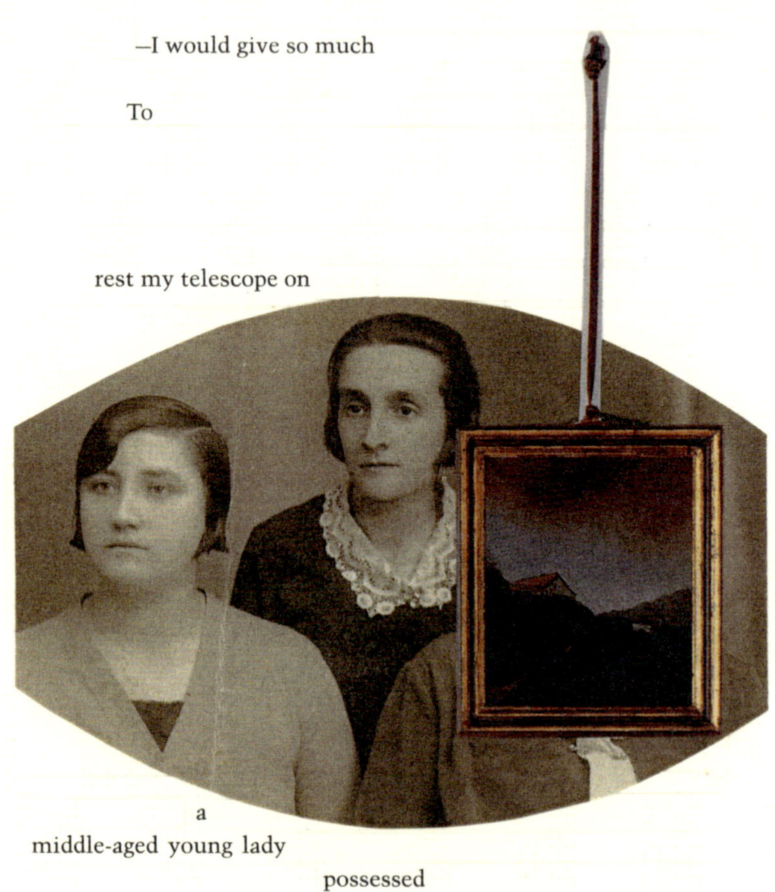

a
middle-aged young lady
possessed
by
doubt-

148

And yet

coolness, and seeming unconcern

in face of the ruin

wrought upon

feeling,

are to me instructive

from the county for theft, he returned to Edinburgh, and was promoted by Brodie a person of the drama. For some time the Deacon had been considering the propriety of appropriating the silver mace of Edinburgh University. It was kept in the College library, where it had caught his eye on the occasion of his visiting with Mr. Smith that seat of learning. So on the night of 29th October 1787 the four partners proceeded to business. "Having got access at the under gate, they opened the under door leading to the Library with a false key, which broke in the lock, and thereafter they broke open the door of the Library with an iron crow, and carried away the College mace." The Town Council forthwith offered in vain a reward for the discovery of the "wicked persons" who had done the deed, and Deacon Brodie was officially shocked at the effrontery of the outrage. The mace was forwarded to Mr. Tasker at the Bird-in-H and the macer thereafter knew it no more.

next victim was an Edinburgh shopkeeper named
Here the usual formula of the Deacon was followed.
ssion of the key was taken, Smith made a false one,
dropped in for a chat with Tapp, with whom, being
am. Meanwhile the others
d secured some nineteen
a miniature picture of a
which picture they broke
it was backed." The jew-
nto Derbyshire, and Mrs.
lis & Horner's shop at the
shall find, far-reaching re-
rodie upon the padlock of
le a satisfactory key, and
and £400 were secured. A
to the detection of the

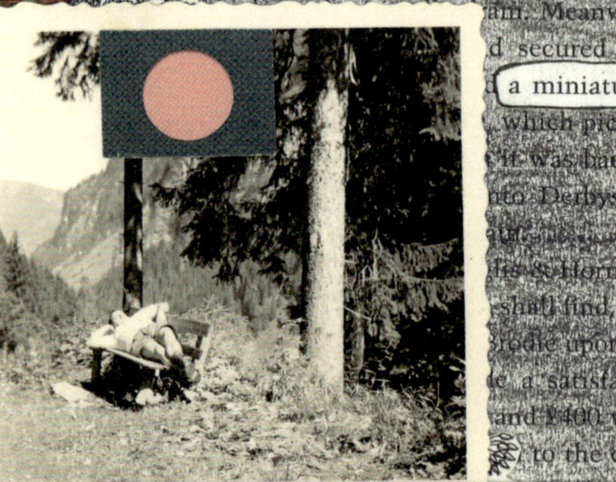

the Crown of

regret

made

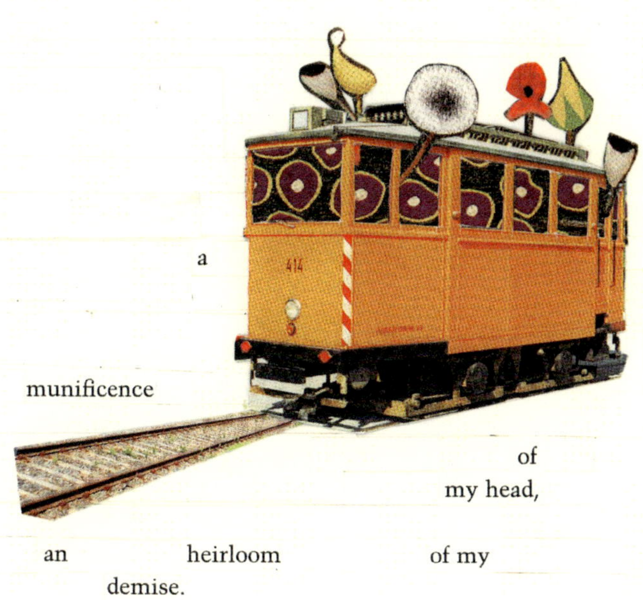

a

munificence

of
my head,

an heirloom of my
demise.

Over a hundred
descriptive writers,

or roughly
52,000 words,

telegraphed in

the opening sentence
that
ushered in the morning

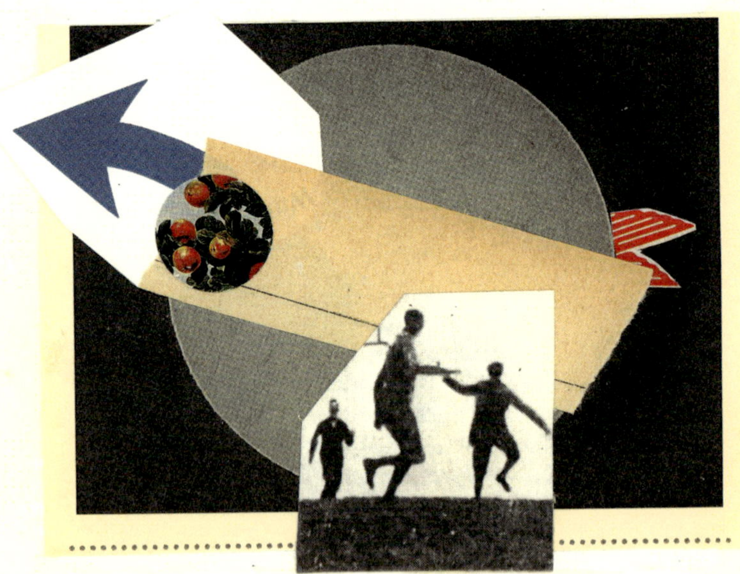

381

internally
life."
was
similar to
the
holy calm
of old newspapers
now impossible to
publish

with subtlety

the dying fire- "retired" to rest,
delivering several opinions on
the
gray vista of the years to come.

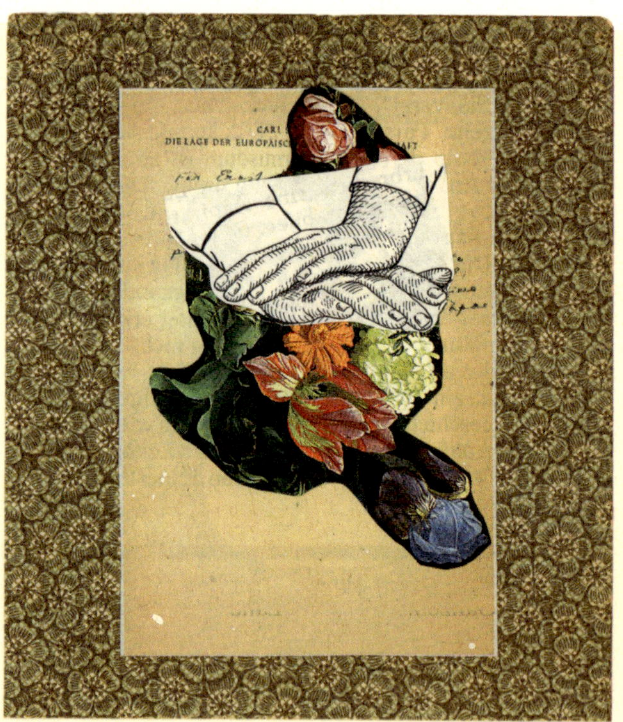

169

Where the skies

weep

by force

the

scene

is

written in a ladylike angular hand,

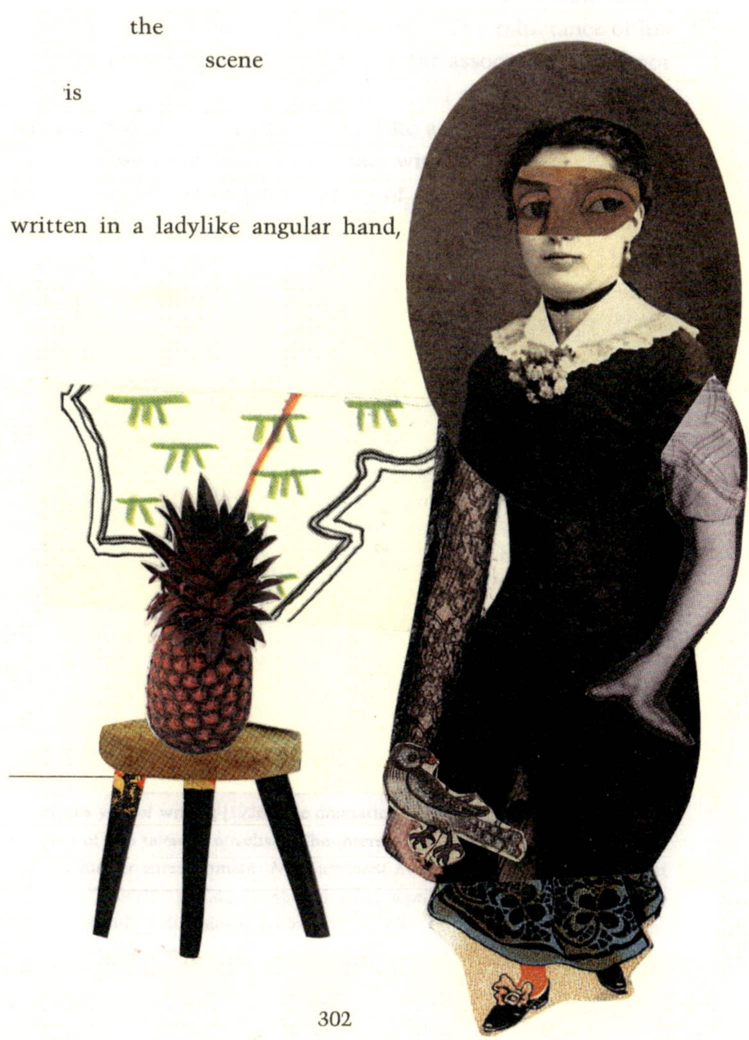

302

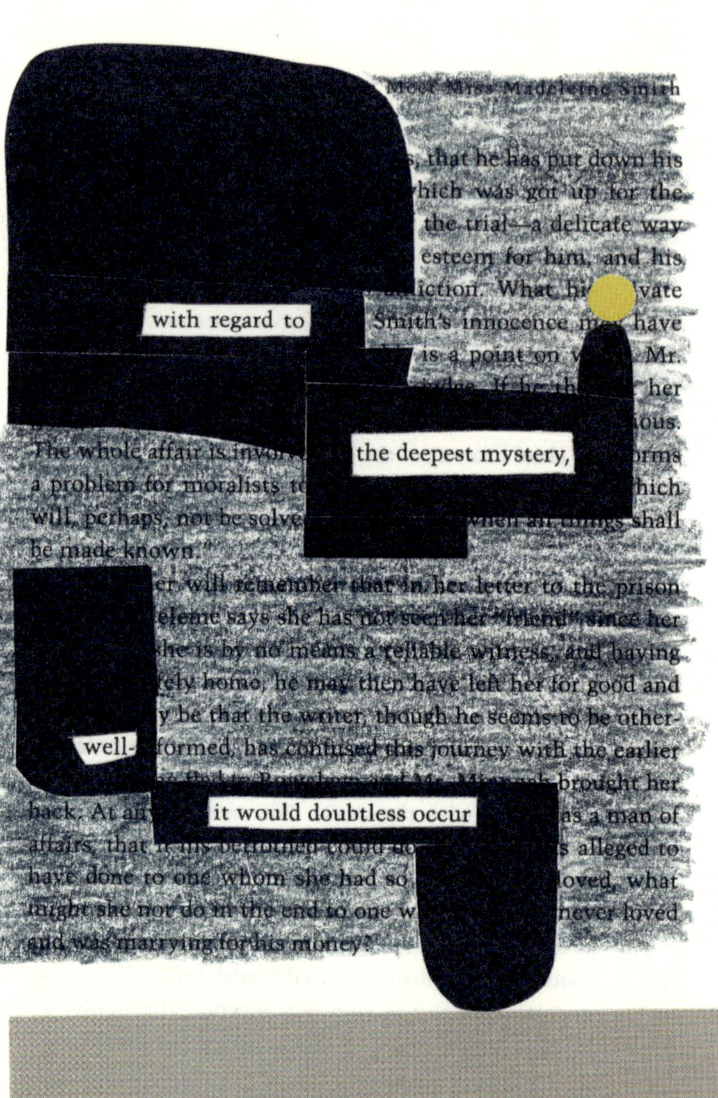
with regard to
the deepest mystery,
well-
it would doubtless occur

163

we

suffered

in the House of Lords

and

the

Lord

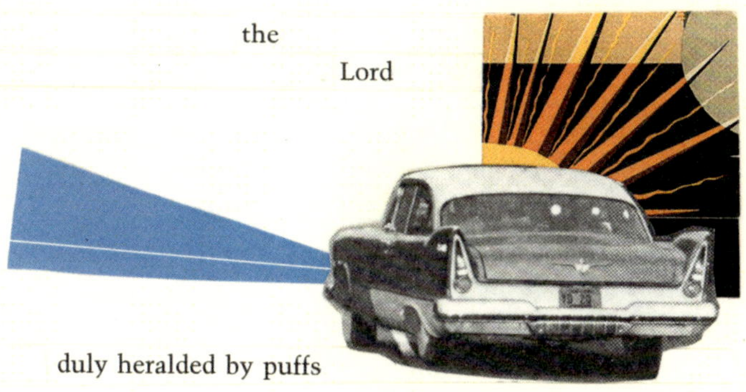

duly heralded by puffs

represented himself to be the victim,

I wonder what

to devote life to

melodrama

ought to be much more effective than it

is

If the flesh is

a profound opera

37

ACKNOWLEDGMENTS

Thanks above all to everyone at Sarabande Books for their support and encouragement.

My gratitude also goes to the readers and editors of the following publications, where some of these poems first appeared, sometimes in wildly different versions:

Ballast, Beaver Magazine, Biscuit Hill, DIAGRAM, Escape Into Life, The Glacier, Hood of Bone, The Hunger, Longleaf Review, Old Pal, Petrichor, $ - Poetry Is Currency, (Re) An Ideas Journal, Shenandoah, Sugar House Review, Surging Tide, and *Whale Road Review.*

NOTES

The poems in this collection are sourced from: Roughead, William. *Classic Crime*s. NYRB Classics, 2000.

The titles of the poems are words or phrases from the respective page from which each poem emerged.

“Secretaire,” the opening cento, is composed of favorite lines from abandoned pieces not included in this volume.

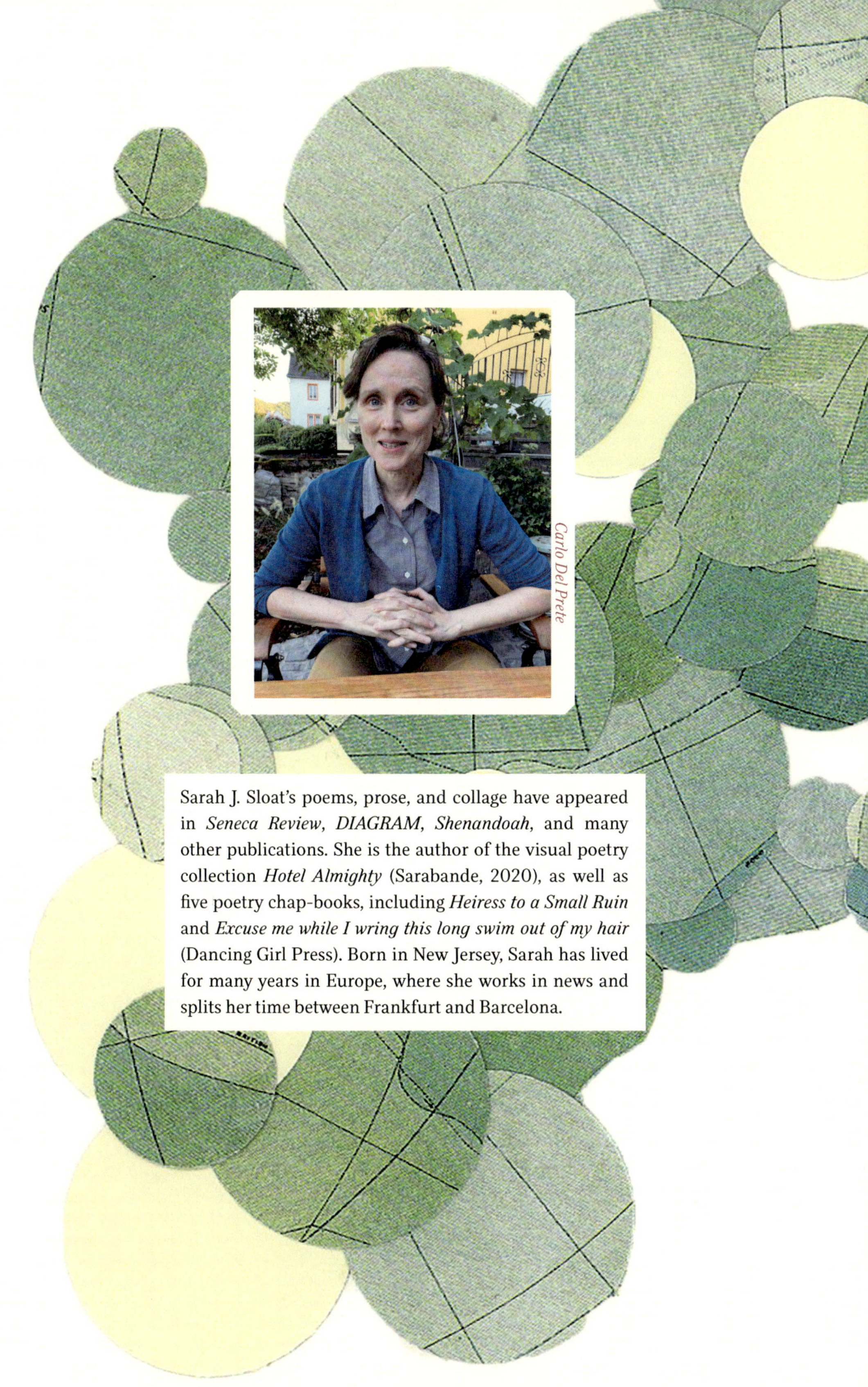

Carlo Del Prete

Sarah J. Sloat's poems, prose, and collage have appeared in *Seneca Review*, *DIAGRAM*, *Shenandoah*, and many other publications. She is the author of the visual poetry collection *Hotel Almighty* (Sarabande, 2020), as well as five poetry chap-books, including *Heiress to a Small Ruin* and *Excuse me while I wring this long swim out of my hair* (Dancing Girl Press). Born in New Jersey, Sarah has lived for many years in Europe, where she works in news and splits her time between Frankfurt and Barcelona.

SARABANDE BOOKS is a nonprofit independent literary press headquartered in Louisville, KY. Established in 1994 to champion poetry, fiction, and essay, we are committed to creating lasting editions that honor exceptional writing. With over two hundred titles in print, we have earned a dedicated readership and a national reputation as a publisher of diverse forms and innovative voices. For more information, please visit www.sarabandebooks.org.

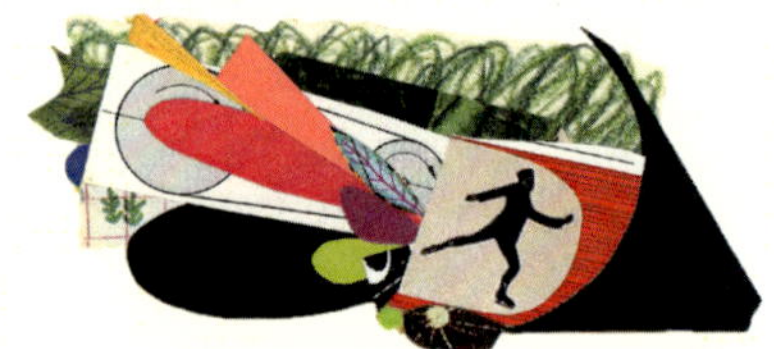